A Silent Scream

~

Patricia A. Yarbrough

PublishAmerica
Baltimore

First printing

ISBN: 1-4241-9251-X
PUBLISHED BY PUBLISHAMERICA, LLLP
www.publishamerica.com
Baltimore

Printed in the United States of America

A Silent Scream

~

Patricia A. Yarbrough

Table of Contents

Dedication Prayer

This prayer is dedicated to you.

Have you had to cry silently? If not, thank God.

Lord, our children are dying younger each year, and we as parents are hurting, you said in your word that anything that's too hard to bear we could give to you, so, God, I'm coming to you this morning lifting the burden off each person's heart who reads this book. God, touch them in a special way and let then know it's okay to cry, it's okay to feel alone, because they're not. You're right there with them. I'm a witness to your presence because without you, there would have been no way, God, for me to make it through this. I give the glory to you, God. Touch these broken-hearted families, give them peace in the midst of their storm. Let them know joy cometh in the morning.

You have to believe, before you can receive the blessings of God. I hope each one of you who had to bear my pain continues to pray and give God the Glory. When you feel like giving up, hold on just a little while longer. If you've made it this far, God will see you through. There's a light at the end of the tunnel and it will continue to shine until you blow it out. It's your light just like it was my light. I blew out my light and your turn will come. Pray and pray; prayers work. Don't be afraid to ask God for anything. Through this walk there are going to be good days and bad days. Continue to pray even when they're good so when the bad comes you're already prayed up.

I personally hope you stay strong and believe. There's light at the end of the tunnel and remember not to give up. I know some of you may feel anger at who I am. I am a survivor after the death of my child and I want you to be, too. May God bless you and protect you.

Acknowledgments

I give my all, my heart, my life, my mind, my soul, my everything to the one and only God. He was and he is the center of my life. He gave me the strength only God could have given. He dried my teary eyes in the midnight hours, He comforted my aching heart, He lifted me when I thought I was at the bottom. I have to say it over and over and over again: Thank you, God.

I would like to thank one of God's angels. I say an angel: she has to be an angel. She watched over me in the midnight hour. She comforted me, she gave me strength. She made me believe in God, and when I wanted to give up on God she made me hold on. I said she made me hold. She told me over a hundred times to recite the 23rd Psalm. Her words were always, "God is not going to put any more on you than you can bear."

Even though I seemed to shut out her words, I heard each and every one of them. She said to me, "God has a purpose for you. He's not going to let you die." I still couldn't understand her loyalty to God. I cried many nights to her. I think at some point she felt was losing me. I was sinking, I was losing my faith, and at some point I even felt I was dying. She prayed with me, when I thought my prayers were going unanswered, she assured me God makes no mistakes.

Every day she would ask me, "How is your book coming along?"

I said, "It's okay, I get the message. Why am I sitting here talking to you when I should be writing?"

Dear Almighty God, I do miss her so much. I couldn't understand how she was praising God when he had taken her grandson. She knew the Lord and she made me know him.

She left here on May16, 1996. An angel, my personal God-trainer, my friend, my mom. She encouraged me every day to finish this book. I miss you so much. I wish you were here. I cry every day, missing you. You taught me how to pray my way to salvation. Your mentor was the 23 Psalm. Mom, I've done that a thousand times in my life after the death of Kenny and now you. I thank God for a praying mom.

I love you mom.

I also want to thank my family. I know you all were hurting just as bad as I was. Even though we rarely talked about Kenny, he was in all of our hearts. I thank God for each and every one of you. A special thanks to my brothers, who stood by me like soldiers. Senior Chief, Retired, Tony and Senior Chief, Retired, Kevin Smith. I love both of you. Walking in that store to buy Kenny's suit was so hard for me: I don't know what I would have done if you weren't there. God will continue to bless you.

Special thanks to my sister, Jack. Girl, you don't know how many days I was hoping you would go home, but you wouldn't. You would stay there all day with me. I remembered one day I pretended to be nodding off, hoping you would get the message and leave, but you said, "Lie down, girl and rest." I gave up trying to send you home. Thank God you didn't leave. I might not have been here today to say thank you. I love you so much and so did Kenny.

Special thanks to my children, Shundra, Julius, Julia and Starla, I love you. If there was ever a moment of doubt of my love for you, I'm sorry. I thank God for all of you. Without you all in my life there would have been no reason for me to hold on.

I thank God for Lil Kenny and Shanae, Kenny's children. I will always keep your dad alive in your hearts. A special thanks to Ashleigh, Branden, Brittany, and Quesean and my newest edition Heavyn. They are the light of my life. They are the light that I saw at the end of the tunnel.

I want to thank a special long, longtime friend. She knew Kenny when he was a year old. She has been there for me like a sister. Joyce, I know many a days I had worn you down and never did you say you were tired. I cried to you and you listened. Even though I said the same thing over and over again. I can't make it. You told me I was going to make it. It seemed like everyone saw I was going to make it but me. I thank God for you. I don't know where I would be if you weren't the supportive, understanding adviser you were. I love you and I thank God for you every day. Everyone should have a Joyce. I do, and I thank God for her today, yesterday, tomorrow, and forever. Thank you for the midnight talks we had. When everyone was sleep, I could always pick up the telephone and cry to you and you would always give me an encouraging word.

I also thank God for a friend named Phyllis. I know you thought I had forgotten about you didn't you. How could I? Phyllis was a play mom to Kenny. Whenever I couldn't find Kenny she knew where he was most of the time laying on her living room floor or sitting at her table. Her son was Kenny's best friend. A friend since elementary school, he was killed in 1988. She had been where I was going. If it wasn't for Phyllis, I would have been lost. Her son and my son were inseparable. When Kenny was shot she had already gotten the word before me and was on her way to the hospital. Her youngest son was with Kenny when he was shot. When I got to the hospital, she ran to me and hugged me. She told me they said Kenny was able to talk. I thank God for her. She stayed at the hospital with me for the entire time, walking the halls with me, listening to my cries. I told her if Kenny died I wanted to die too. She kept saying Pat you can't you have a husband and other children to think about. I didn't want to hear that. I felt so helpless but she never left me.

I remember one night when someone said somebody got shot in the area where all the children were hanging out, Phyllis and I both jumped into our cars, wondering if it was our child. No one knew who was shot but they knew Kenny and Kevin were in the area. Someone had come and done a drive-by shooting. We both met at the same time at the hospital in the middle of the street. We both ran over to the children who were already lying on the ground crying. We asked who had been shot. Before an answer came here came Kenny and Kevin. We both were relieved but still concerned. I hugged Kenny so tight and she did the same.

Our hearts felt the same pain then and now that we both have lost Kenny and Kevin. Phyllis you're a special lady, a loving lady and a mother to many of the young men who departed this life. I cried to Phyllis for months telling her day after day I wanted to die. She said it was going to get better but I couldn't see how. I do today and I want to thank you Phyllis, for being a million moms.

Special thanks to another special lady in my life, Sharon. I owe you a part of my life. Sharon was a play aunt to Kenny. She's Phyllis' sister. She too, had made it to the hospital to be with Kenny before my arrival. I remember when I first got to the hospital she also assured me Kenny was talking. She said she didn't get to see him. But she told the doctor she was a relative and that she is.

Sharon walked the hall with me for at least twelve hours. I cried to her, telling her, "Please don't let Kenny die!" She said to me, "He's not." I felt so helpless, I felt like a child. She wiped my face as quickly as the tears streamed down my face. She told me it was okay to cry. She said she knew how I felt; she felt the same way when Kevin died. Every day after Kenny's death she continued to tell me, "Trish, it's going to get a little better day by day." Even though it took years, I want to thank you, Sharon, and I want you to know I love you, and may God be with you.

Pastor Donald Weathers, you know I wouldn't and couldn't forget you. I thank my Lord and Savior Jesus Christ for you. I cried many silent tears in your presence. You gave me support in every way possible. All I ever wanted to do you helped me accomplish, and that was to open a center for parents and siblings of murdered children. You took time to help counsel the wounded mothers and children every Wednesday. Even though you had not lost a child, you stood by us to the end. Your counseling was the greatest gift you could have given me. You showed us we have to let go and let God.

You helped my mind, and body and a lot of other peoples'. God is good and is love, and so are you. Continue the good work, Pastor, as God has chosen you to. Giving me the Wednesday night for all of us to come together was worth it all; it was the best thing for me. Those sessions were healing me through Kenny's death and the death of my mom. Thank you and again and God bless you. I love you.

I would like to thank God for the congregation of Galilee Baptist Church. A special thanks to Minister Gayle, Minister Francine Singletary and Minister Donna Warren.

I would like to also thank a very special friend. No matter which road I was to take she would follow. The many nights we attended our weekly meetings she was tired but she always managed to be there, tired and all, waiting to do whatever she could to help me. Patrice Parrish, my friend, I want to thank you for being there in the midst of the storm. If she could have cried for me she would have. Anything I was trying to do in healing of others, she stood waiting to be the first to assist. Again I love you, Patrice, and thanks.

Chapter 1
The Night Of

On a cold night in December 1989, at age thirty-five, my life should have been just beginning, but instead it ended. My son, my baby, Kenny was shot. My daughter and I were going home from work. She had a part-time job with me, to earn credits for her senior year. It wasn't an unusual Friday night; police were racing up and down the road for whatever reason.

This particular night was a little unusual. It wasn't quite 7:30, yet five or six police cars raced past me, almost hitting my car. One came an inch from hitting us. I decided to follow him but I changed my mind. I think now to myself, if only had I followed the police car, I would have found out they were racing to the scene where Kenny had been shot.

I went home to the most devastating news in my life. My daughter Julia (Pooh as everyone knew her), was waiting by the front door, crying and frightened to tell me the most heartbreaking news of my life, Kenny had been shot. My world as I had always known it ended that night. Nothing would ever again be the same. My husband had already gone to the scene to be with him.

I thought of this little bundle of joy I once held in my arms now lying in the street drowning in his own blood. Just the thought was enough to make my heart stop. I never thought anyone would hurt him in this manner. I never would dream of anyone wanting to hurt kenny.

All I could say was, "Dear God, no." My daughters jumped in the car. My body began to shake as though all of the muscles died. I screamed silently. I never made it out of my car. I backed out into a one-way street, almost backing into a police car I did not see. My thought was with all the police cars I saw racing up the street, there weren't any left. Then I realized he was on his way to my house. He put on his flashing lights and I stopped. I don't think he thought I saw him. I don't remember if I did. My thoughts were on Kenny, and why was he coming this way anyway.

He stopped his vehicle and walked toward me, and then I realized he was our neighborhood police officer who knew Kenny. He asked me if I had heard the news. I said, "Yes" and asked how he was. His voice and the look on his face gave me the answers I needed. Not good. He said, "It didn't look good." I died then, at least a part of me. The only thing that held me back was the sad little faces that sat in the car with tears streaming down their little faces. How could I let them see me in that state of mind? I knew they wouldn't understand.

I got out my car and walked over to the police car, screaming silently. The officer called up to the scene on his radio and asked if I could come to the scene. They said no and my heart stopped again. I thought Kenny was dead. As he was on his way to the hospital I screamed silently. While they were talking I was praying Kenny was alert enough to hear and to know it was me who was calling.

He asked them to what hospital they were transporting him. They said, "Prince George's General Hospital." I wanted to leave my car and start running. The thought was there and so was my husband, pulling up in front of the police car. He looked saddened, confused, and distraught. He tried to hide it, but I knew him well enough to know by the look on his face things were not good. He told me to take my car home and ride with him. I don't how but I parked. All I could think about was Kenny. I had just talked to him less than four hours ago. A part of me died at that very moment. I wanted to run and scream, and lay down in the middle of the street crying tears that would flow forever and ever. I wanted to run in the front of a moving car so that my heartbreak and hurt would be instantly over. I screamed Kenny's name silently.

My body was as numb as ever, with tears streaming down my face. I quickly got out of my car and into my husband's car then the kids got in and we left. I was missing a child, Julius, my youngest son, but I also had a shot child waiting on me. I had to make a tremendous choice. I left and prayed God would watch over him while I went to the hospital. I was hoping he didn't find out before I got to him.

You know how news travels and of course he got the news. I was devastated to know he had received that harsh of news without me being there to comfort him. I know when I got the news of Kenny being shot I indeed needed my mom.

On the way to the hospital, the ride was quiet and tense. Everything and everybody seemed to have gotten in the way. I wanted to jump out of the car and start running, even though my husband was already driving over the speed limit. I became nervous and wanted him to drive faster. The thought of Kenny being shot raced through my mind and again I screamed silently. I began to wonder if he was scared or in pain. I know he needed me and God knew I wanted to be there. The thought stayed in my mind, how bad was he? I knew he was afraid of needles and I knew they had started an IV. I cried again. But this was a time neither of us had a choice. If I could have just been there, it would have made a difference to him and me. The thought of him going through this alone made me scream. I know God was with him. He had to have been.

Arriving at the hospital, I saw a helicopter in the path. I stopped and stared in disbelief. The fright Kenny must have experienced. He had never flown a day in his life. The motherly thought "Was he taken care of?" and so many other thoughts raced through my mind. The one that carried the most, "Was he in pain?"

Oh God, please don't let him die. I remembered looking at television when people were being flown in by helicopter and seeing how well they were taken care of. I hoped that was true, at least for this time.

We pulled around to the visitors parking garage. I couldn't wait for the gate to come up. I wanted to drive through everything. I needed to be there with Kenny and traffic seemed to be crawling. My skin felt like it was too much for my body. I wanted to be free to fly to be beside my son. Even though I was walking as fast as I could, it felt as if I was not moving at all.

We reached the emergency room. Once there I saw two of Kenny's friends. They ran over to me and threw their arms around me and I began to cry. They went to the front desk to let them know I was Kenny's mom.

Within seconds, the door opened and so did my heart. It was a doctor in a white uniform. He told me all the things I wanted to hear, and gave me hope. I later found out they were all lies. He led me to believe Kenny was fine. Yet I couldn't see him. His response was they were trying to stabilize him, which meant more than the words coming out of his mouth. He convinced me he was alert; he knew my name, and my work number. I said to myself, okay let me hear those words, then they will mean something. I didn't, I couldn't. The doctor was talking to me as though I was listening; without a warning I passed out. All I could remember was something strong being given to me. The smell of it was very strong and it smelled like ammonia. I heard my children cry out "Oh my God, my mom!" I was ready to let go. I no longer saw those little sad faces I saw death.

Two doctors exited again, heading toward me. They seemed to be walking in slow motion. Time seemed to stand still. In my heart I knew this was it. Kenny was dead. My heart was pounding faster than I could breathe. The news they were coming to tell me was Kenny was on his way to surgery. He wanted to let me know he was the one I should talk to find out about Kenny's condition at any time and I could pick up the telephone on the wall next to the operating room and he would try all he could to abreast me of his condition. I nodded my head and sat down and continued to cry.

Chapter 2
The Next Eighteen Hours

I didn't know if my mom knew. I didn't have a chance to call her. I knew if my sister found me my mom had to know, she tells her everything. I sat in the lobby with my husband, sisters and friends. My mom and my brothers were there in less than two hours. My brothers had to have been speeding, because the trip from Norfolk usually took three and a half hours.

The lobby was filled with Kenny's friends, young and old. The love showed. It poured out in numbers and tears. The sad faces of his friends hurt me even more. I was sitting between two of his friends or play moms Sharon and Phyllis. They had been where I was going. They had lost a child and a nephew. I knew if anyone would understand and know the pain, they would. I was scared in my own body. I was shaking uncontrollably. I sat for a second and then I walked the floors for hours. I wanted my mom. I cried myself to sleep. When I woke up for the second time, I looked up and there she was.

I ran to her and buried my head in her chest and cried so helplessly. I knew she understood my pain and hurt. Kenny was her baby. She raised him while I was in school. He thought I was his sister and my mom was his momma. She had him spoiled rotten, he knew it, she knew it, and so did everybody else.

She wanted to know his condition; I shared with her what they had told me. Her first instinct was to pray. We all prayed together.

My mom held me close to her and began praying. The more she prayed the more I cried. My brothers and sisters drove from Virginia Beach to be with me. I thanked God for all of them. I needed them and continue to need them in my life. Coming from a family of fourteen children, we are very close.

The room was filled with my family; they had to take turns letting each other have a seat. Some were already on the floor in the corner with their heads buried crying. I couldn't sit so I walked the hall crying and crying. Passing Kenny's friends, they put their heads down in sorrow. Yes, it was sorrow and it was also pain. I continued to walk the hall, crying. At some point I was openly crying about my child; a part of my very soul was lying alone, fighting for his life. I thought back over the years when he had fallen off of the pool table, how bad I was hurting, how I cried then. The thought then made me cry now, realizing that was minor considering my cries now.

I walked over to the telephone and called the doctor to find out if there was a change in Kenny's condition. My mom kept saying no news is good news. I tried to believe that, but it was too hard. I was wondering what was taking them so long.

I looked up at the clock nine hours had passed and Kenny was still in the operating room. I waited and waited and cried and cried.

It seemed as though no one understood my cries. I sat quietly in the corner alone. I needed to meditate; I needed peace; I needed to understand why, what could have gone wrong. I asked if anyone knew what happened. Someone told me Kenny and two of his friends were walking on a path to the store. I couldn't believe that. Knowing Kenny he would never walk on a dark path. I was asking myself over and over again, why Kenny? I couldn't find peace. Everywhere I went there was someone staring at me, or wanting to hug me. I thank God for all the love and attention I got. I needed every bit of it. Yet I needed answers.

With all I had gone through for the past ten hours, I began to have difficulty breathing. I thought about Kenny already in the operating room, fighting for his life. What if I died and Kenny lived, how would he make it? He always told me if I died first, he couldn't make it, and neither could I. I had no choice; even though a part of me was giving up I had to hold on. I was taken to the emergency room. I couldn't stay, I was afraid the doctor would come out and I wouldn't be there. All my thoughts were about Kenny not about me. I screamed silently and raced out of the emergency room, back to where I sat until the doctor came out.

At age five he was ready for kindergarten, but I wasn't. I didn't want him to be away from me. I took him to school on the first day. I cried instead of him. He was only there for a half-day. He rode the bus home with his cousin, who was the same age, Freda. I couldn't wait until twelve o'clock came. I would be standing in the doorway at 11:55. Don't let the bus be late! I would walk outside and stand until it was visible, about ready to ask the bus driver what took so long. Instead as long as I saw my baby I was happy. Every day he would bring me home a picture of something or someone. Half of the time I couldn't tell you what it was. I said, "That's pretty," but to myself I thought, it would be pretty if I knew what it was. Within an hour of my return to the waiting room, the doctor came out. He looked exhausted and the look on his face frightened me. I felt my heart stop beating; I felt like I was going to die. My husband and mom and other family and friends stood behind me. I didn't want anyone to hear what the doctor said to me. I guess that was selfish; not so much selfish as afraid. I wanted to scream; I knew my screams would affect everybody. I stood quietly and patiently waiting to hear about Kenny's condition.

The doctor began to tell me about Kenny's condition. My scream was again silent. He said, "Kenny died twice on the table," and so did I. I began to hyperventilate again. I couldn't leave now; I had to hear about Kenny. I wanted to push him out of the way and run in the operating room with him, where he lay as helpless as I was. My son needed me more than he ever would and I felt as though I died. Here was a hurt I did not have the power to take away. I felt lost and alone.

I was crying silently for a second, but within minutes my cries were no longer silently. They pierced the long hallway I had seen for the past eighteen hours. The sound of my cries made others cry.

Some of them had not heard anything other than my cries. Some thought Kenny had died on the table. I walked into the waiting area which was now filled with many of Kenny's friends. Many of them were cuddled up in the chairs together; some of them were outside sleeping in their cars. With my appearance they all gathered together to find out how Kenny was. I felt I owed that to them.

Many of them had been there as long as I had. After telling them what I knew there were more screams, more cries. I wanted nothing more than to close my eyes and wish and pray that this was a bad dream. The constant sounds of cries helped me know this was real. The doctor told me he had severe bleeding of the right lung and that had to be removed as well as a part of his colon. He would have to undergo at least two more extensive surgeries before it was over. Kenny was extremely critical. Even though all his family and friends had been there for the past fourteen hours, they could not see him because of possible infection. One hour per day was all I could have to spend with him. I felt sad not to allow his family and friends to see him. The more he told me the more I wanted to die. I knew there was no chance for Kenny pulling through yet, I prayed anyway. The doctor walked away after telling me the first twenty-four hours would be critical, and so was I. He said if Kenny lasted through the next twenty-four hours he would be out of danger. I began counting the hours and praying. I counted twenty three hours from the time it came out of his mouth. I stayed four more hours with nineteen more hours to go. I prayed, "God, please let him live for the next twenty-three hours, please." Every minute was a valuable minute. Every half hour, every hour.

I cried openly and silently. He had said it would be another hour before he would be taken to his room. Then I could see Kenny. I sighed, I was speechless, devastated, heart broken. You name it, it was me.

My body became so limp I wanted to drop to the floor and scream. As bad as I wanted to let go I had to hold on. I couldn't do it. Because in an hour I would be able to see Kenny. I had to hold up. I did. I thanked the doctor for all he tried to do. I knew he had given his all.

I could see it in his eyes. He wanted to save every part of Kenny he removed. I know he did. He showed good faith. He wasn't responsible for what someone else did. I couldn't fault the doctor. He did his job. I thanked him again and again he nodded his head as though he wished he could have done more. I walked away crying, this time openly. The sounds of my cries brought more screams.

Kenny's best friend was his cousin, Gary, who kicked the wall and punched in the glass of the fire alarm. When the news broke about the severity of his wounds, more cries, echoed throughout the waiting room. It had already been thirteen hours and not a soul had left. Kenny's son was there at the hospital. I held him so close and kissed him. I whispered in his ear, "Your daddy is going to be all right." I knew the love he had for his son. He was only three months old, and the thought of him never seeing his father brought more screams. I gently whispered into his ear again, "Your dad loves you." I hoped that stayed in his head forever.

I gave the baby to my mom and I left to meet Kenny on the second floor, which was the critical care ward. That was where he stayed for seven days until the day he died. That was also the day a part of me died. Nobody could understand my cries unless you have walked this lonely road to hell.

Nobody else was allowed on the floor at that time of the morning, other than my husband and I. Of course my mom didn't want to hear it, so she came in on her own. She found me. I had left her with the baby.

Before I realized it she was walking slowly down the hall. You couldn't separate her from Kenny. We sat quietly in the lobby. Every little noise I heard I jumped up, Thinking it was the staff bringing my child. It wasn't him; it was another patient coming from the operating room. I sat down for another ten minutes, and I heard another sound. This sound was louder, and people were talking and I looked over the chair and yes, it was finally Kenny, being wheeled down the hall. They had him hooked up to what looked to be a thousand machines. They knew I wanted to see him. Just as they got close enough to me, they slowed down. Tears began to run down my face, the pain, the sadness took over my tired body. I wanted to push them out of the way and grab him and tell him to wake up. I couldn't so instead I sat and cried silently. My heart couldn't take it anymore. I knew for sure I wanted to die. I asked God, "Why me? What had I done so awful in my life that my child had to be shot." I never got an answer, because there was not one. I was not being punished, it was God's will, but at that moment, I just did not want it to be done.

The nurse told me as soon as she got him situated in the bed, someone would be out to get me, and I could come back to be with him. I shook my head and walked way. I had already been at the hospital at least fourteen hours. My body was tired but I was not going to leave the hospital until I saw him. If it meant another fourteen hours, I would have been there. I sat in the waiting room and did what I had been doing, for the past fourteen hours, prayed, cried and wished this was just a bad dream. I sat and waited. I needed to go somewhere and scream until I couldn't anymore. I did but silently. I screamed for hours it seemed; there was nobody there who could hear me, but it is a sound I still hear. It was heart breaking even to my own ears, the silent screams.

Before I knew it Kenny was ready for sixth grade. He was still adorable. Big brown eyes and still my baby. I loved him so much. The next step was junior high school. He was quiet and didn't have a lot of friends. He would come home from school and lay in front of the television. I wanted him to mingle but he wasn't ready. I didn't dare push him. Those two years in school flew by too fast. He was in middle school when he began to open up a little. His dream was to play football. He based his life on it. He loved the Dallas Cowboys, and his idol was Tony Dorsett. Every Sunday he would lie in front of the television waiting patiently for football to come on. He would halfway look at the other teams, but he was a true Dallas fan. If they won, he praised them and if they lost he praised them.

An hour or so had gone by and no nurse or doctor had come out to let me know I could go back to see Kenny. I got up but my body stayed there. I walked to the critical care ward where Kenny was taken.

The nurse looked up and asked if she could help me. I glanced over to see them changing his bandages. I wanted to run over there and grab him. I couldn't take it anymore, watching someone taking care of him other than me. That was not what I was accustomed to seeing. The nurse was in the room and asked me to wait five more minutes. I wanted to tell her no but I said quietly, "Please help save my son." The thought of those five minutes seemed to be another lifetime.

Just as I was leaving, heading toward the door, the nurse taking care of him, told me it was okay, I could come back to see Kenny. For the first time in eighteen hours I was about to see him. I walked over to where he was laying and I screamed silently. "My baby! God!" was all I could say. I stared at him, no not Kenny. My eyes reminded me and I said, "Yes it is him." I walked closer to him and touched his hands and feet. They were so warm. I touched his forehead and rubbed his legs. I just wanted to touch him forever and ever.

My husband was on one side of the bed and he was rubbing his hands and trying to be strong for me. I was too hurt. I couldn't cry. My body was shaking uncontrollably; what was I to do? I felt as helpless as Kenny did. I wanted to do more, but there was nothing I could have done except pray as I had been for the past eighteen hours.

The pain, that weight on my heart, made me feel like I was going to die. I couldn't breathe. Maybe I was feeling what he was feeling. He was hardly breathing since he had one of his lungs removed in surgery. He was hooked up to a respirator which was doing seventy-five percent of the breathing for him and I was doing the rest. If I could have given my lungs to him to breathe I would have, and he knew it. I stayed at his beside for another thirty minutes or better. I whispered in his ear that I was going home to shower and I would be back later. He shook his head no, so I stayed. To leave him was the last thing on my mind. I wanted to stomp, scream, and say wake up! I couldn't there were too many people around. I sat down next to his bed and stared at him in disbelief. I couldn't believe what my eyes were seeing. Calling his name was all I could say. I said it over and over again.

While sitting there the door opened it was my mom. She wasn't supposed to be back there but he was just as much her child as he was mine. I gave him birth and she gave him life, especially if she felt he needed her. I couldn't tell her she couldn't be back there even if I did she wouldn't have paid me any attention. She prayed over him. I know he heard her. He knew the Lord. When he lived with her, they had to go to church on Sunday. To know Kenny, you had to love him; he was that type of child.

Chapter 3
My Thoughts

I walked the halls of that hospital so many times, back and forth. I know I left my footprints on the floor. I prayed Kenny would be all right, so one day we could walk back over those same footprints; back down that long hallway, to that same cold room where I spent twenty-four hours waiting for him. I wanted to share that with him. I wanted to show him where many of his friends slept in chairs, cuddled up under one another. I wanted to show him the fire extinguisher his cousin Gary broke. I wanted to show him the front of the building where cars were lined up from one end to the other. I felt there was so much I wanted to share with him. Something could have been a past for the both of us. I wanted to let him know so many people loved him. I had no doubt I wasn't going to be able to share that with him. I knew Kenny was going to live.

As I was walking down the hall, all sorts of things were racing through my mind. What was he thinking about when he was shot? Did he call my name? Was he cold when he was lying bleeding to death on that cold pavement? I would never know. So many thoughts, and questions I would never know. So many thoughts and questions, but no answers surfaced my mind. I don't think I will ever again have a peace of mind.

My mind was going on and on. People would be talking to me and I would be looking them right in the face and not hearing anything they were saying. My mind was on Kenny and the person who shot him. Why? How can you shoot someone and go home and go to sleep? How could you? I asked myself over and over again. I couldn't get an answer and still to this day I don't understand. I guess I would never understand. Young people were dying in the street; the sound of gunfire makes my heart skips a beat. Mothers are screaming why but receiving no answers to their cries. My son; who made the choice he should die. Young men are dying in the street. How could you kill and then fall into a peaceful sleep? Do you care about the hurt you caused, the sense of loss?

The misery his family must be feeling, the loneliness his family must now have to deal with the silent tears a mother cries, the ways she slowly dies inside. Who gave him the right to take Kenny's life, I ask, why?

I am more than sure they slept through the night, while my child fought to live. What kind of people were they? Kenny's dreams and mine were shattered. The thought of no more Sunday football games with him, no more coming home to him laying sprawled in front of the television as though he owned it. At this moment, I was thinking and crying silently. Would we get to do these things again? I hoped and prayed we could still watch football together. We both were Dallas fans. I looked forward to every Sunday when Dallas played and we would watch it together. He would be in his room and I would be in the kitchen, probably cooking. A good play would happen and he would run up stairs and ask, "Man, did you see that?" He was always so happy, with the smile of a loving child. I smiled as I thought about the good times and I cried silently as I thought how he lay in the hospital fighting for his life. I was fighting for my life, to be strong and believe he would be all right.

I shook my head and continued to walk the hall, crying silently. My body hurt. I could barely stand to be touched. When people hugged me it hurt, even though it was meant to be comforting.

Chapter 4
The Day After

I left the parking lot of the hospital, for the first time in eighteen hours, I saw the light, smelled the fresh air, saw cars moving and realized I had not died. I walked toward the car. I felt the door handle. It was cold but it was real, and helped me to know that life was real outside the hospital.

Reality came back when I passed the helicopter area. It made me realize this was not a dream from which I could wake up and escape the fear of death. Reality and not a dream it seemed too cruel to be real. I could not take my eyes off the scenery. I began to visualize a scene where the helicopter had landed, and nurses and doctors were running out to meet him at the helicopter landing. It was like something from television. I beat myself up so bad, and it hurt. We passed through the light and I left some of the thoughts that were once on my mind back at the hospital. Why Kenny? was a thought that still haunts me to this day.

The ride home was as quiet as the ride there. This time I knew where he was, and that he was being taken good care of. No one could hurt him now. I dropped my head and began to cry. I no longer had a silent scream. My oldest daughter, Shundra, reached across the seat and rubbed my head, while the other children bowed their heads. They did not know what to do and neither did I. Everyone remained quiet all the way home; my husband lit cigarette after cigarette until we got home. I normally complained about his cigarette smoke but now his smoke didn't faze me. I guess he was happy not to hear my mouth. I was hoping Kenny didn't wake up and find me gone. I just wanted to go home and lay my body down for a minute.

Even after the eighteen hours of being in the hospital, I could not rest yet. I felt if I pretended things were all right, it would make everything okay. Hoping this was just a horrible dream, I could open my eyes and it would go away. I knew in my heart that no amount of pretending could change the harsh reality that awaited me at the hospital. Kenny had to hear my cries even at this distance.

Arriving at home, I had to drop the children off, as much as I didn't want to go home, as much as I didn't want to go to the house. I had to run to the post office and mail my life insurance check which was in my purse the night Kenny was shot. I never realized the check was in there until I had to give the hospital his insurance card. At the thought of another tragedy in my life, I screamed. What if Kenny died? How would I be able to bury him with this check in my purse. I cried, "Oh God, please don't let Kenny die." I needed to get to the post office and I needed Kenny not to die; both were very important to me. I drove to the post office; put the check in the mail and prayed this wasn't the okay for Kenny to die. I never really thought he would die so it did not faze me. After talking to the doctor earlier at the hospital, reality hit. The doctor said Kenny was in a touch and go situation. I then realized the importance of my insurance check.

After leaving the post office, I drove home with Kenny still heavily on my mind. I ran upstairs to the bathroom, shut the door sat on the floor, and cried my life away, asking God, "Why? What had I done, God, what?" I couldn't think of anything Kenny or I could have done that would have placed something so tragic on either one of us. I had began to question my faith, my belief in God. I began to wonder if there was a God, and if so where was he. I needed him right now. Little did I know he was right there with me, every step of the way. Who else could have helped me after surviving a child being shot to death? I tried to hold on to my faith, but it was fading and so was Kenny. In my heart, I knew when darkness was all around God would carry me into the light if I needed him to, but my mind wouldn't let me think that way. My child was fighting for his life while this other person was at home sleeping. I screamed silently.

A knock on the bathroom door let me know my cries were no longer silent. It was my mom. She held me close to her and told me to pray and hold on and remember that God is in control. I said, "I can't, Mom, it hurts too bad." I felt like a child, crying and holding on to my mom. She never left me, and neither did God. In her arms, I received comfort from a loving heart even though I knew hers was breaking just like mine. She continued to pray and believe that God was going to see me through.

I told her I wanted to take a shower. I don't think she believed me. She went into my room which was next to the bathroom, and waited for me. I turned on the water, got in the shower, and cried and screamed, and didn't care who heard me. I was devastated. My child was lying in the hospital fighting for his life for no reason. Kenny should not be lying in the hospital. He should be on a football field, riding a dirt bike, partying, having dinner with his friends, he should have been in the kitchen with me having dinner, yet instead he was laying in the hospital fighting for his life. The smile he always had I could no longer see it. There were so many things he should have been doing. Because of someone else's choice there my child lay, fighting just to take a breath. Why? I would give my life just to hear his voice once more.

What did I have to be so secretive for? I didn't have a reason, but I had many reasons to scream, and lie down and die if I wanted to. It wasn't my call; it was God's call, and it wasn't for me to decide whether it was right. I cried for twenty minutes before getting out of the shower, crying, begging Kenny to hold on. As lost as I ever have been in my life, I screamed. Getting out of the shower was the last thing I wanted to do. I wanted to let the water run forever. Staying in the shower meant not having to talk to anyone, hiding the sad look on my face. Hiding from the world that awaited me when I opened the door. I couldn't face coming out of the bathroom. I opened the door and a brisk draft of cold air chilled my body. I knew I hadn't died. I looked as though I had been in a fight and lost. My eyes were sore and so swollen and red from crying I could barely see. I wrapped in a towel and walked into my bedroom. My mom was sitting on my bed and she helped me dry off as she did many a times when I was a little girl. I was lying across the bed for about fifteen minutes, scared to death that my telephone would ring. I lay there wondering if there had been any change in Kenny's condition. Wondering if he had woken up looking for me. I was wondering if they were taking good care of him. Just thinking about Kenny caused me to look up and scream silently. I felt trapped in my own body. I wanted to run, I wanted to scream forever. I wanted so bad to pick up the telephone and call the hospital. I was afraid of what I might hear. I wanted to know the truth but I was afraid to hear it. The last thing I wanted to hear was Kenny was going to die. I screamed silently for minutes, hours, day, nights and it seemed no one heard my cries.

Chapter 5
Seven Days; An Escalator Ride to Hell

An escalator ride to hell. That's what it had been for seven days. From the time Kenny was shot until the day he died. Seven days of hell, back and forth to the hospital morning, evening and night I prayed.

Day 1, he had been in surgery for nine hours. I was tired and my body was ready to shut down yet I stayed at the hospital until I was able to see Kenny. Going home it was no longer a home for me for the next seven days.

The thought of it all made me cry. If it depended on his love for me, I knew he wasn't going to die. I held on to the thought of our love for each other. I thought about the promise we made to each other when he was three years old. He promised me he would never leave me.

I held on to that promise, and I was hoping with every breath in my body we could keep that promise. Knowing how bad he was injured, left me with little hope, yet I held on anyway. I knew no matter what I wanted, God was in control. I had to believe in him. I was afraid, even though I held on, believing God was in control, and it's a mother thing, you know.

The hospital staff knew more than they wanted to tell me, or they weren't sure, either what was going on. After spending nine hours in an operating room, dying twice on the table, yes anything could happen, and it did happen. Kenny was dying right before my eyes, yet

I couldn't see it. I may have seen it, but I didn't want to believe it. Who would want to think their child is dying? No one, not even you. I had been up for the past twenty-four hours sitting in a cold hospital, screaming silently. The chairs were so hard that when I stood up, there was no circulations in my legs. I didn't care. All I cared about in the world was Kenny. Nothing else was a concern. I hadn't eaten or drank anything for the past twenty four hours. I wanted nothing but to be with him. My body felt as though it was ready to shut down. It did; my legs went numb and my body began to shake. I was dying too and didn't know it. I hadn't been to sleep in the past twenty four hours. I never walked so much in my life.

Day 2, I was at home thinking about the good times we shared. I dozed off and the telephone rang. I jumped up instantly. It was the hospital, Kenny's nurse informing me he had taken a turn for the worse. I needed to get over to the hospital right away. I asked myself, "What could be worse than where he was, lying there fighting for his life, hooked up to a respirator, heavily sedated, tubes in his nose, a tube in his throat, and a catheter to help him urinate." "What else," I asked myself, could go wrong?" I wanted to run; I wanted to lie down and die. Instead I screamed silently and prayed that God would comfort me and take away the pain and hurt. I cried, "Dear God, no! Kenny can't die." I called my husband and told him what the hospital said. We all began running around getting dressed. We left immediately. I was shaking and crying, saying, "Dear God, please don't let Kenny die! Please." I was afraid he was going to die before I got there. I knew if it depended on Kenny he would wait for me. I knew he loved me and wasn't ready to die. I continued to think about the good times we shared together. I knew Kenny was going to hold on even if it meant asking God to wait for me. Time was important for me and Kenny. I needed to get to the hospital.

I headed toward the door with my purse on my shoulder, barely able to carry my body any longer. I felt tired and ready to give up. The thought of Kenny lying in the hospital gave me the energy I needed to walk out the door. I opened the door slowly. I screamed silently. I wanted so many times to scream as loud as I could. I couldn't; there were my children who needed me.

33

I didn't want to stop at the lights. I wanted to run them. Everybody seemed to be driving slower than usual. We dodged a few lights by taking the back roads. My heart was beating just as fast as the car was moving. I kept praying and asking God, "Please don't let Kenny die; I'm on my way." I prayed if never he heard my cries, please hear me now.

We reached the hospital. I wanted to get out and start running but the car was still moving. I couldn't wait to park. It was too hard. I needed to get out now. Soon we stopped. I opened the door and began to walk ahead of everybody. This is my child I had no time to wait. I didn't want him to die alone. I wanted to be there with him. I pushed the elevator button but it seemed forever to come. I wanted to take the steps, but I knew my body wouldn't allow it so I had to be patient. I couldn't but I did. I had to calm down. The steps would even hurt my feet. No one could touch me, it hurt for any one to touch me. My body was inflated with pain. I hurt all over.

When arriving on the floor where Kenny's room was, I headed straight to the back. Before I could reach his room here comes the doctor. I wanted to run the other way. I wasn't ready to hear he died.

Instead he put his hands on my shoulder and walked slowly back to the lobby with me. My legs were limp. They were about to let me fall. We sat down and he put his hand on the top of mine. He looked me straight in the eyes and said to me, "Kenny may have to go back into surgery." Every breath of air in my body left me. "If he does, he won't make it, he's too weak," he said. "An infection has set in his body, and as I expected I will have to go in and operate." I died right before his eyes and he never knew it. My mind went blank. For a second I didn't see or hear him anymore.

He said the next twenty-four hours will be very critical, and so was I. I put my head in my lap and began to cry. My mom and my husband stood by me. I couldn't take it anymore, I asked God to take me. The pain was too much. I couldn't believe the spiritual saying God would put no more on you than you can bear. How could I believe it, when the weight of the world was already on my shoulder.

I wasn't about to leave the hospital. I sat in the lobby wondering what was Kenny thinking about. Was he thinking about me and was he in pain? Every time I heard a stat call I almost started running. I knew a little amount medical terminology so I knew there was an emergency situation. I sat in the chair rocking back and forth. Wishing the world would go away. I couldn't eat, I couldn't think, I could do nothing but rock back and forth praying that God would see me through. It was another three hours before I could see him again. I sat by the entrance. I wouldn't leave. I continued thinking about the good times. I knew God wasn't going to let him die. I wanted so bad to think of all the good times, but I couldn't. I couldn't even smile.

We had some good times. He was my best friend. He was my son. He had a knack for scaring people, but he didn't like to be scared. I remember one day I had come home for lunch from my job which was less than five minutes away from my house. I saw his car in the driveway. I opened the door and called his name, but he didn't answer. I figured he wasn't in the house. I opened the mailbox took out the mail and sat down on the chair. I sat back for a second just to stretch.

As I was looking at one of my bills a hand touched me on my shoulder. I screamed, jumped up and ran to the door. Before I could open the door, he said, "Man it's me." I turned around speechless. I said, "You better stop playing so much before you get hurt!" He laughed. I didn't finish my mail; I took it back to work with me and read it there. I told him I would not come home anymore. I grabbed my purse and headed toward the door. He walked me to the door, laughing. That's why I knew he couldn't die.

My body felt as hard as the chair I was sitting in. I knew the chair couldn't move, but I had to stand up; my body was heavy from the silent screams. It was full of fear that I was going lose Kenny. I walked back and forth, wondering if this was just a bad dream. Was I going to close my eyes to wake up to a bad dream? Unfortunately the door opened and the doctor came out again and so did my heart. I could look in his eyes and tell it was over. I knew Kenny had lost the battle. I didn't want to believe it, but it was reality.

My son, my life, was over. He came over by me and again I

wanted to run and scream. This time he told me he was stable again for the moment and the fever had gone down. I was screaming silently, as so many times before. I looked at the clock. It was 6:55, five minutes before going back to be with my baby. As much as I wanted to, I couldn't cry. It hurt so bad but the tears wouldn't come. I guess God knew I had a much rougher road ahead. God protected my poor aching heart. I could have died and I wanted to so many times, I said yes and God said no. I now know how powerful God is.

God is good no matter how we look at it. The situation may not be the way we want it, but believe me, there has to be a God for us in a time like this. I should have been dead, I could have been and through the grace of God I'm still here.

My husband and I walked down the hall holding hands, trying to be strong for each other, knowing this was a very difficult time for both of us. We continued to walk, holding hands. I wanted to scream knowing we were only a few feet away from Kenny's room. I took in a deep breath and walked with the weight of the world on my shoulder, screaming silently as I headed toward the door. The closer I got the more faint my heart became. I didn't want to go back there to see him like that. I wanted to run away forever. I knew Kenny was lying there fighting for his life and so was I.

Kenny was asleep, as we had seen him before. I wanted to hug him. I could only touch him gently. His body was extremely hot. I became exhausted just at the thought of his body temperature that hot. I removed the cover from his feet. I rubbed his feet and they were a little cooler. I guess I wanted to believe they were. I cried silently at the end of his bed, wondering if he knew I was there. I wanted so much for this to be a bad dream, I stared in disbelief. I couldn't believe it was Kenny, not Kenny laying there. I cried and cried begging God to let him be okay. He had such a bright future ahead of him. He had told me two weeks ago, starting the first of the year he was going to attend barber school. He wanted to cut hair and I wanted to do nails. We had a plan to open a shop. The thought made me cry even harder. I managed to smile a little at that thought, but soon the smile turned back to the saddest smile in my life. I never gave up hope.

I couldn't understand again why Kenny. Was I dreaming? I began to meditate to God, asking him to please not let Kenny die. I never left the end of his bed. I wanted to jump on the bed and hold him forever. I wanted to scream, "Kenny please don't leave me." Instead I screamed silently. This time tears start rolling down my face. I was getting weak, I was getting tired, and I was ready to give up. I wanted to die before Kenny. I began to feel he was going to die. I wanted out first, but God said no. I felt that was my choice but God saw differently.

Visiting hours were only an hour long. I had already spent forty minutes rubbing, praying, and trying to comfort a child who was so critical. I knew I had to leave in about fifteen minutes, but I stayed for the entire, hour and plus. The announcement came over the intercom that visiting hours were over. I cried silently and said to God, "I can't go." He gave me the strength to go and believe in him. I put my head down and walked out of the room, thinking, am I going to see Kenny again? Why Kenny? This stayed in my mind as I walked the long hallway. Each time I walked that hall it seemed to get longer and longer.

Before I decided to leave the hospital, one of the nurses came over and informed me she would be Kenny's nurse. Her name was Kelley and if I had any questions I could call her anytime of the night. I thanked God for her, to know that someone was going to be there with him. She gave me her number at the desk. I guess she saw this sad face so many times before. I took the number and headed toward the door. She rubbed my shoulder and said, "Call me anytime you want." I said, "Thank you." God is good through the midst of it all. I left with relief, knowing someone else cared about Kenny. I cried silently, leaving the hospital. I continued asking God, "Why?" silently.

I remembered how Kenny was one day. He had to stay in the hospital for one day because he had a bad throat infection. He didn't want me to go home. I had to leave him, and then I was sad. I had to get home and get the other children ready for bed. I called him as soon as I got home. He was acting like a baby at age seventeen. I went back up there around eight o'clock. He wanted me there. I stayed until eleven o'clock. I gave him a kiss and left. Before I could get in the door he had called. I wished for that time instead of this. Sometimes we don't understand how blessed we are. Sometimes we complain and don't even realize how blessed we are. I wish I could have that day back.

The road home was quiet, knowing God had chosen someone to watch over Kenny. I wish I could have been the one God had chosen to stay with him.

The thought of going home was a nightmare. How could I go home and leave him? I began to wonder, what if Kenny woke up and found me gone? Was he thinking about me? While in the front seat of the car I was crying silently at the thought of Kenny lying there fighting for his life. A teardrop was in the corner of my eye, waiting to roll down my face. I quickly pretended something was in my eye and wiped it away. The kids and my husband were in the car. I was concerned about my strength for them. What about me?

Once arriving at the house there sat Kenny's little red car that he loved. Nothing fancy, just a car. I stared and stared until my stares became noticeable. We pulled into the driveway. The kids and my husband got out and I stayed in, staring at the car with tears rolling down my face, praying when I opened the door he would be in the house.

The pain at the thought of Kenny probably never coming home to drive the car drove me to scream silently. I sat for another minute or two with my heart racing 120 miles, and then I tried to get out of the car.

My body was heavy, not from weight but from tears, grief, and pain at the thought of Kenny laying in the hospital fighting for his life. I looked up only to see my mom standing in the doorway, looking so helpless. I knew she wanted to do so much more, but there was nothing she could have done. It was all in God's hand now. Whether he lived or died was left totally up to God. I tried hard to convince myself God was going to see him through, but the injuries to one lung, and a part of his colon being removed; those things would not allow me to believe anything other than Kenny would die.

The house was full with friends, relatives, and people who loved me. I began to wonder if God was punishing me. For what, I asked myself? I have always tried to do the right thing. At a time like this you tend to want to blame someone. The one at blame is the person who pulled the trigger.

I've always helped people. I did anything and everything I could to make anyone happy, even if it hurt me. I asked God, "What did I do to deserve this?" No answer, only tears streaming down my face. I walked into the kitchen and so many faces looked down, hurt and sorry as though what could they say, what could they do to help me? They did right. They kept silent while I screamed.

Day 3, I was at home, sitting in the living room, thinking about Kenny, when the telephone rang and my heart jumped. I thought it was the hospital, but instead it was the police officer informing me they had the people who shot Kenny. I was happy yet I was sad. What good would it do? If Kenny died there would be no justice, only if he lived. He told me they were in jail in the District. They had committed another robbery the same day, this time a car jacking. The car they were in flipped over. At least, I thought, they didn't get shot. They aren't hooked up to a respirator; they aren't fighting for life, only Kenny was. I was thankful that at least they couldn't hurt another child, another family.

He was going over to the jail to visit them. I wanted to ask for what. I had to remember Kenny was my son, not his. He had to have them extradited to Prince George's county. I wanted more than anything to see these people. I wanted to be face to face. I wanted them to know how they destroyed my life. Not that they probably cared. I wondered if their parents knew what they did. I know as parents we can't always know what our children are doing while in the streets. Love starts in the home. I wondered how a child could be so cold and uncaring about life. Were they scared knowing they could spend the rest of their lives in jail? How did they sleep after shooting my child and running away, leaving him dying on the street?

The officer wanted to see me on Thursday around 1 p.m. to discuss the case. He informed me there were two witnesses who actually placed these people at the scene? He hung up, and I went back over to the table and sat down in the living room with my family. The look on my face told them something was wrong. I told them who it was on the telephone and what the police said. My mom started praising the Lord. She said, "I told you God would take care of you." I thought to myself quietly, What about Kenny?

I didn't want to spend my time thinking about the call from the police officer; I had something else to think about; Kenny. Kenny was my everything. These guys were his everything. He had his job cut out for him.

He promised to meet with me tomorrow. I wondered what kind of people they were. How could they shoot anyone and go home, close their eyes, and go to sleep? I didn't understand how they could be so cold! I wondered what they looked like, not that that would make a difference. I wondered what kind of family they came from. There couldn't have been love in the home, or discipline. There was something missing in their lives and now mine.

The police officer told me they were sixteen and seventeen years of age. They were old enough to know better. They wouldn't want to be shot and left to die. What were they thinking when they shot Kenny, robbed him of his coat in the middle of December, and ran, leaving him not only dying but cold and drowning in his own blood?

Day 4, Thursday morning came, and I thought about what I had to do. I was to meet with the police officer. It was frightening to go to a police station. I had never been there before and pray to God I will never have to go there again. It's scary to be down in the basement with a cell. I know I couldn't or wouldn't be able to live in something so small.

The detective handling the case was very concerned. He told me he had visited Kenny earlier at the hospital. He was also upset from what he saw. He had hoped Kenny would be able to tell him something. He said Kenny was not able to provide him with any information because of his condition. I screamed silently. I knew the condition he was in. He said to us he had a suspect in custody in the D.C. jail and was waiting on him to be extradited to Prince George's County.

He asked me when I went to the hospital today to take a picture of Kenny. I asked why, and he said in the event Kenny lived he would have a before and after picture to show the jurors. I said okay. He told me he had Kenny's clothing in a bag, and I asked him if I could have them. He said, "You wouldn't want them in the condition they were in. They were bloodied and cut up because the paramedics had to cut them off." I cried silently. Maybe if I had cried out instead of silently it would have made a difference. Who knows if it would have?

The telephone rang, and my heart jumped out of my body. I just knew it was the hospital calling, but it turned out to be my job calling to see how I was doing. I thank God for their concern, but all I wanted to do was scream. I talked very briefly. They were very supportive; I can never thank them enough.

I went upstairs to my bedroom and fell across the bed, crying openly for the first time. I cried to Kenny. I begged him, "Please, Kenny, be strong. I love you, I need you." I cried and cried. Today was not the first time I said, Kenny, I love you. We always exchanged those words. I never felt anything in my life that hurt as bad as this. It felt as though someone snatched my heart out of my body, the pain, the loss, the loneliness. I can't explain it. I wanted to die. I couldn't think of what it would feel like to lose my child, my best friend. I couldn't, so I cried. I was lost not knowing where or which way to go.

My body was tired; I hadn't eaten or drank anything in the past twenty-four hours. I thought neither had Kenny. I was wondering if he was hungry, knowing how much Kenny liked to eat. The thought made me cry even harder. I lay there so helpless, with my mom rubbing my head. It was not my head that was hurting, it was my heart. It was broken and hurting bad. I continued to allow her to rub my head while I screamed.

I knew visiting hours would be coming up shortly. I had to change clothes and shower.

I tried to get up but my body wouldn't move. I scooted down to the end of the bed and allowed myself to fall to the floor, crying. My mom was holding me close to her, assuring me God makes no mistakes. I couldn't relate. My child was laying there from gunshot wounds to the chest, missing a lung, part of his colon removed, a kidney removed, hooked up to a respirator, and she was saying to me God makes no mistakes! I knew my mom meant well, I just couldn't understand.

I managed to get up to make it to the bathroom and showered. As the water poured over my aching body, so did my tears. I cried and cried, hoping no one could hear me. I cared about who heard me. I've always been the strongest of fourteen children. I couldn't break down even if I wanted to. There were four little children of mine who were depending on me for strength; there was a husband who was trying to be strong for all of us. How could I think about me?

My body was still in shock. I knew what I needed to do; I needed to pray. I tried to, but my body said no. I couldn't fight anymore. I had no trust in anyone, not even in God. I was hurting. Only God knew the pain I was in. Yet I couldn't cry to him, I was too angry. I, too, was dying like Kenny. I had the motherly instinct he was going to die, and so was I.

While trying to rest my body, the telephone rang and it felt as though my heart jumped completely out of my body. I screamed silently. It was the hospital; Kenny had again taken a turn for the worse. I was talking to the nurse and the doctor got on the telephone and said he may have to take Kenny back into surgery. I sighed for a second. If he did, the chance of him surviving was zero. Tears started rolling down my face. I said, "No, God! Please! Why?" The doctor insisted we come over to the hospital immediately. Also Kenny's temperature had risen to 104. I knew then it was over. I remember how I saw him yesterday so swollen and warm from the infection in his body. Why? That was all I could say for the moment.

I walked calmly downstairs and told my mom what the doctor said. I couldn't rush because my body was so heavy from tears. I didn't care anymore. I wanted to die. I felt it was the only relief for me. I grabbed my coat and keys and left, wondering if I was going to make it there before he died. I did not dare share that with anyone. How could I?

Back to the worst place I didn't want to be. I couldn't take it anymore; I laid my head back on the chair and let my tears have their way. Everything felt as though it was shutting down. I was losing control. My life was slipping away right before my eyes, and I did nothing to stop it. The thought of Kenny dying was all that stayed on my mind until I got to the hospital.

The drive seemed to be getting shorter, basically because I knew where I was going and I didn't want to go there. The only good which came out of the trip to the hospital was I knew Kenny was there and still alive. I looked forward to walking into his room in spite of the noisy machines he was living on, in spite of his inability to talk to me.

Every day I would sit next to him rubbing his hands and feet and watching the machines which kept him alive and praying and screaming at the same time, hoping tomorrow I would come in and find one of the machines gone. Instead I found everything as it was from the first time he came into the hospital. The only thing that changed was they put him on another bed which rotated his body. He couldn't move so they didn't want him to get bedsores and to keep the fluid from building up around his one lung left. I was concerned about how they transferred him from one bed to the other. I prayed they took care of him. I know sometimes nurses and doctors can be cruel. I was hoping they didn't lift him the wrong way and he was in pain. I wished I could have been there. Of course I wasn't. Sometimes I think God didn't want me there since he was there.

The thought of the respirator hooked up to Kenny made me sad. This long tube was in his throat. I wanted to breathe for him. The respirator was breathing for him seventy-five percent so he was doing very little on his on. Every visiting hour I was hoping to see it go down. Only once did it go to zero. With the removal of one of his lungs, the doctor was trying to strengthen the other lung in the event he made it.

Arriving at the hospital, before I could get to the room, Kenny's doctor and two more doctors were in the hall talking. Kenny's doctor had his back turned so the other doctors continued to talk. They had never met me, and they were discussing Kenny's case. I found out one doctor was from the insurance company. I guess his concern was how long he would be in the critical care ward. They wanted to move him to their facility. Like I cared about how much it was going to cost them! Hell, it was costing me something more valuable than money; Kenny's life.

At the sound of my footsteps, Kenny's doctor turned around and realized I was there. He introduced the other doctors to me. I nodded my head. They all told me Kenny was a fighter. They couldn't understand how he made it this long. I guess they didn't know God was in control. One doctor said to me with injuries of that nature, he should have died the night of the shooting. I cried silently. That's what hurt me so bad, knowing Kenny was not ready to die.

The doctors wanted to move Kenny to another hospital if he became stable. I became confused. One minute they were saying he was in a touch-and-go situation, now they were saying to move him to another hospital. I was confused. Then I realized why the other doctors were speaking of moving Kenny. It was for insurance purposes. I didn't care about their financial part; my only concern was Kenny getting the best of care.

I became very angry after realizing why they were there. They were not concerned about the patient, they were concerned about the cost. I began to cry. This was not the time or place for that conversation. I walked away in disbelief. Their concerns were about the amount of money; mine was if my child was going to live or die. One of the doctors proceeded to say he did not know how Kenny had survived this long. I looked down and said to myself. The reason is because you are not God. To look at the extent of his injuries, he should have died the night he was shot. I screamed silently. I too, though that, but God had the last say so. I became so sad knowing Kenny was not ready to die.

That was why he was still holding on.

I knew he wasn't ready to die no matter how everyone tried to convince me he was better off dead. Those were fighting words to me. What right do people have telling you something like that?

After listening to the doctor I knew Kenny was going to die. He seemed as though he was trying to soothe a wound that was already too deep to heal. I wanted to ask him to tell me the truth, but I knew only God had the truth.

I wanted the truth but I didn't know if I was ready for it. You know, I know the truth is what we all want, but can we deal with it? No, because it hurts. I was already hurting and dying. What more pain could be inflicted on me?

He began telling me a mother's nightmare. Kenny was in a touch-and-go position, meaning it could turn either way. Yes, he could die. Those were the words he would not say for five days. There was no more assurance from the doctor. He, too, had put it in God's hand.

I was still holding on, praying that Kenny was going to make it. I wasn't ready to put it in God's hand even though it was the right thing to do. I just couldn't. I had a very selfish love for Kenny; I wanted him to myself. I know God has a purpose for each one of us, but I wasn't ready to give him to God. I needed him.

God knew and that's why he took him. If it was up to me, Kenny could have lived in the hospital forever and I would have been right there every day watching over him as I did for the past three days.

I waited for the next visiting hour. I needed to spend every second with him. At 6:59 I headed toward Kenny's room. I wanted to just look at him. I needed to hug him. I wanted him to hear my screams; I wanted the world to hear my screams, and Kenny was about to die. After all I just heard from the doctor. I wanted to look at him forever. I walked into his room and I stared and stared as though I was never going to see him again.

I didn't know if my last look was today. Only God knew, and I was hoping he showed me a sign that what the doctor had said was not true. The sign was right before my eyes,

Kenny was still living.

Visiting hours were almost over. My mind became as hard as a rock. I couldn't move, I couldn't think, I couldn't do anything but ask God. Why?

I left Kenny's room to go home. I wanted to stay for all of the next visiting hours, which would have been tomorrow. I felt there was no place for me to go. The lights were being turned off and every sane person was on their way home. I felt I no longer had a home.

I sat my tired body in the chair. I couldn't move all I could do was cry. So many times I cried out to Kenny, asking him to hold on. I rocked back and forth with my head buried in my lap. I have never felt as helpless in my life as I did tonight.

The security guard was walking the hall, informing everyone visiting hours were over. For some apparent reason he bypassed me. I was too hurt to care about him. I thank God he passed me. I sat for another half hour. I lifted my head and told my husband I was ready. Not ready to leave the hospital but ready to leave this world forever. I had given up hope. I wanted to die.

We walked slowly toward the elevator. My husband had to push the button. I had no strength. I had nothing. The elevator door opened. I became like a child and didn't want to get on. I didn't want to leave Kenny. I wanted to stay there.

The elevator door opened to the first floor to get off, and I stood there. I couldn't leave.

What was I going to do at home? Kenny needed me. I know he did. Where was home? I felt I had nothing.

I stepped out of the elevator and walked slowly to the car. I couldn't even open the door. My son was in front of me and he opened the door. After putting one foot in the car my body fell into the seat. I was feeling like a rag doll.

After everyone got in the car, I turned around and said to my kids, "I love you but I can't take anymore." Their sad faces made me hurt even more. I didn't know what to do. I thought for a while I was going to die before Kenny.

Our ride home was as usual, quite. No one knew what to say. Even the youngest wouldn't talk. Most of the time when they didn't understand what was going on they would continue their talkative moments, but not this time. I wondered if she understood her brother had been shot. I think she knew but understanding the severity of it was the real answer. She was only six years old. The next to the oldest was sixteen and I had a set of thirteen-year-old twins.

It wasn't all about me. I felt I was dying, but I knew these kids needed me. I had no life in my body. I was just living, living for what? My child was in the hospital fighting for his life from a senseless crime. I felt I was being punished, the children were being punished, and my husband was being punished.

We all were hurting, so senselessly. We were about five minutes from the house and I knew the children had not eaten so we stopped by McDonalds for something to eat. I had not cooked since Kenny was shot, and I didn't know if I would ever want to cook again. After getting their food we had a very short distant to go home. I did not want to go there. I wanted to run away and never see that house again. We turned the corner and there was the house I hated so much.

Even though Kenny was holding on I knew he was in danger; I felt it. You, being a mother, have also felt danger for your child. You knew something was wrong but you did not know what.

The children went to the table as I have always insisted. You eat at the table, not throughout the house. I had to get away. I went upstairs and laid across the bed in disbelief. My child, shot three times. I buried my head into the pillow and cried and cried, soaking the pillow, continuing to ask God why.

My heart was broken. It felt as though it had been ripped out of my body. I managed to carry my tired body down to join my family. As soon as they heard me coming down the steps I felt all eyes were on me. No one ever knew how I felt. I hid my emotions as much as I could.

It was now day number five, and nothing had changed as far as Kenny's condition. I had to now depend on prayer. I had given up on my life. My only concern was Kenny. I put everything I had into hoping and praying he would come back home. I did not feel that was asking too much. That was where he lived, that was where he belonged and that was where I wanted him. The question was, what did God feel was best for Kenny?

I finally got down on my knees and prayed harder than I ever had before. I knew no matter what or how hard I prayed God had the last say so, but I did it anyway. I felt what did I have to lose. I felt I was already losing a child. I cried and I prayed and cried and prayed.

I could barely get up off the floor. I was so tired. It was the longest ten minutes of my life. Only God knew what I had been through, what I was going through, and what I was about to go through. If only my family knew the pain their sister, aunt, wife, and mother was in. I do not think any of them would have been able to go through what I was

47

going through and still keep their sanity. It took more than one person to handle the burden.

Losing a child or facing the possibility of losing a child is truly a burden. I do not ever want to think of another human being enduring such pain as I have in the death of my child. I tried to do it all by myself. Why? Because I was afraid of letting people know how bad I was hurting. I felt I had to be strong. I later realized I had no reason to be strong. I had every reason to fall to my knees and scream forever. Yet I kept quiet for my family and the children.

Getting back to the fifth day, I was sitting on the sofa and the telephone rang. I started to run out the door. I couldn't take any more calls from the hospital. Thank God it was not for me. It was for someone else in the house. I sighed with relief. I was nervous every time the telephone rang. I knew it would be the hospital. An hour went by and I began to feel a little relief. Maybe Kenny was doing better. Damned if that old devil tried again to steal my joy. The telephone rang again and this time it was the hospital. My sister called me to the telephone. She stood right there staring in my face. Never did she realize I was screaming silently right before her eyes.

I talked with the nurse and she insisted I come over to the hospital and bring my family. I knew it was over. Kenny was dead. I knew it. What else could there be? She wanted the entire family. I wanted to go alone. They would not allow me. I wanted to die. My faith was gone, and so was my desire to hold on. I was getting weaker the closer we got to the hospital. All I could think about was Kenny. I repeated to myself, "Kenny, hold on, I am on my way." I figured with no faith I had no chance. I guess God knew he was my only strength. He was the only one who knew what I was going through and what I was feeling. He knew.

Once arriving at the hospital, I wanted to jump out of the car and start running and not stop until I got to Kenny's room. I needed to run somewhere. It was taking too long to get out of the car. I needed to get away.

There were people in front of me, in back, and on the side of me. I had nowhere to go. I walked casually like everyone else. If only they knew I felt I was running even though I was right there beside them.

We got to the elevator and I did not want to push the button. I did not know what to expect. I died right before my family's eyes. I know I did. A body that has no life has to be dead. I was only walking, talking, and holding on, through the grace of God.

The elevator door opened and so did my heart. As I was stepping off the elevator heading toward the critical care ward, here came Kenny's doctor and two other doctors. I knew it was over. I could not do anything. I felt so lifeless, so saddened thinking about my child, my best friend.

His doctor knew what I had been through for the past ninety-six hours. He knew the many calls I had received. He was tired and so was I. I had to hold on, but he did not. He did not have a child in the back fighting for his life, only a patient. I had much more than he, yet he was very caring. To look at Kenny you had to have a heart.

He was such a beautiful child. The doctors came over and sat down beside me and told me again Kenny was still in a touch-and-go situation. He could go any minute or he could live. Basically what they were telling me was my child was going to die. I sighed for a moment and tears began rolling down my face. I asked myself, God why me? Why? I cried knowing that Kenny was not ready to die. That is why he was still holding on.

They went on and on talking medical terminology. They told me if he lasted through the next twenty-four hours, there was a possibility he would be out of danger. I began counting the hours and praying. I counted twenty-three hours from the time those words came out of his mouth. I did not leave the hospital for four hours, which meant I had nineteen hours left. I kept saying to myself, "God, please let Kenny make it through these next twenty-four hours, please."

Every minute was a valuable minute, then the half-hour, then the hour. I was beginning to feel a little hope. Eight hours had passed and Kenny was still alive. I almost believed he was going to beat it. My spirit had been lifted a little. I was feeling a little better. No telephone calls from the hospital. I had called the hospital; even though the nurse told me nothing had changed, I took that as a blessing, Kenny was still living.

I even tried to sleep a little, remembering what the doctor had said about if Kenny made it through the next twenty-four hours he somewhat had a chance. I was already at eight hours. The telephone rung, I jumped up so fast I got dizzy. It was my sister calling. I lay there thinking. You shoot someone, leave them on the ground to die, take their coat off their back, and you continue on a rampage. I shook my head. I had to worry about Kenny. I was still facing a tragedy. Kenny was not out of danger yet because of these kids. I needed my strength; we still had fifteen hours to go. I could not spend time worrying about the person who shot him.

The police wanted to meet with my husband and me in the morning. I felt I had no time for any one. I needed this next fifteen hours for nobody but Kenny. I tried not to but I had to go to the police precinct in the morning. The night was going by okay. Kenny was still holding on and so was I.

Morning of Day 6 came too fast. I did not want to meet with the police. I was afraid of what I had to face. I got up. Before I could lift my head off the pillow I reached for the telephone and called the hospital. I began to think Kenny had died and they forgot to call to tell me. The nurse answered the telephone and knew my voice. She said nothing had changed through the night. I sadly said, "Thank you." I was happy Kenny was still here with me.

The house was full of family members. But yet I couldn't talk. My entire body felt so empty, so lifeless. I sat down and laid my head back. Thinking about Kenny, tears began to stream from my swollen, red eyes and down my face. And before I knew it my pillow felt like someone had poured a bucket of water on it. I talked to my mother and told her the police officer had wanted me to take pictures of Kenny. She wanted to know why. I explained it to her and she could not respond either. He had visited Kenny early, maybe Wednesday morning, and he too said he was sadden Kenny was not able to talk with him. That was the reason for the picture, in the event Kenny survived. There would be a before and after picture for the jurors to see. The thought of me taking a picture broke my heart.

I went alone. I felt this was something I needed to do. On the way to the hospital I thought silently. What a pleasure. I felt everything was going just fine. We were already less than fifteen hours away to a miracle. I reached the hospital very early.

Day 7, I continued counting the hours. We still had fifteen long hours to go. And they were long. Every time the telephone rang it shortened the hours. I just knew every call from now on would be the hospital. I even asked my family and friends to refrain from calling unless it was absolutely necessary.

The nurse was expecting me. I had called prior to coming. She felt it was okay. I wondered what she knew that I didn't. I entered the hospital with more joy than I had in a week. I pushed the elevator button to the third floor and walked down the hall hoping this day would be the best day of my life. I opened the door to the critical care ward and the nurse on call looked up. She smiled and I walked over to Kenny's bed. His curtains were drawn and I saw a pair of feet. I stepped back and said I was sorry. He said, "No problem, come on in." I asked who he was. He stated he was from the dialysis department. I asked why he was there. He said Kenny's kidney wasn't functioning. I looked startled and asked why someone didn't consult me if this was to take place. He said it had to happen or Kenny could die. The kidney wasn't cleaning the blood like it should.

I looked down at the bag attached to Kenny. I thought he had urinated. I was happy to see urine. Within minutes the technician said he did it for him. I cried. I had been waiting for six days to see if Kenny could produce urine on his own. Unfortunately another downfall for me. He said he would be finished in about ten minutes. I wondered if Kenny knew I was there. According to the doctor he did. He was lying so peacefully. I stared at him, as I never had before. Kenny, I kept saying to myself, this can't be. Yes it was, and this was the seventh day.

He said I could stay if I wanted to. Of course I did. He would be done less than ten minutes. I had come to take pictures and leave. He walked out. I walked over to Kenny's bed and whispered in ear, I'm here. As much as I wanted to scream, I couldn't. I know he knew I was there; I wanted him to acknowledge me. He was still heavily sedated, which he had been since surgery.

The second day in the hospital the doctor had told me to talk to him, even though he seemed not to hear me. I told him I loved him. I walked to the end of his bed so that I could get a complete picture of him. I wanted every machine to show. I wanted the jurors to see how Kenny was suffering and how I had to live, how my family had to live. The entire family was affected by this senseless shooting. I asked myself over and over again why me, why anyone?

I looked at the respirator Kenny had been on since the shooting. It was still breathing for him seventy-five percent. That had not changed since he had been in the hospital but once. Once when I went there and it was at fifty percent, I was happy. After taking the pictures, I rubbed his hand, and kissed him on his forehead. He looked so pretty. His complexion was beautiful. I was excited at how good he looked. I drove home feeling the best I had since Kenny had been shot. Oh God I was happy. I couldn't wait to get home to share the news with my mother. I didn't realize this was going to be the worst day of my life.

I was so excited I went to visit a friend of mine named Debra. I couldn't wait to tell the world how good Kenny looked. I felt everything was going to be all right. She knew him since he was a year old. I was going to call and tell her, but her telephone was off so I went to her apartment. I shared the good news with her. We stood in the middle of the floor hugging each other and crying over a child we both had known for nineteen years. We had been friends since the ninth grade. She walked over to the table and picked up a photo album. We looked through and found pictures of Kenny she had from when he was a baby. We both smile and talked about the good times with Kenny. I thought to myself Kenny can't die, too many people are praying for him.

I held on to that thought for another day. We sat and talked for about fifteen minutes. She wanted know how I was holding up. I said I was holding on. We hugged. I knew I should be going home in case the hospital had tried to call me.

Just as I was about to leave for home, my pager went off. It was my house with a 911 in my pager. I figured it had to be an emergency if they put 911. I hurried out the door with my friend. She walked me to the car; only to find out I had a flat tire. I had to walk to the store at the corner to call my husband to pick me up. I was only three minutes from the house. I knew whatever happened I would be there in minutes. My husband came to fix my tire and another page went off, again 911. This time I got scared. I knew something must be wrong.

I ran across the street to the nearest pay hone and called home. My mom said, "The hospital called." I said, "Okay, I'm on my way."

Since I was only three minutes from home, I should be there; I drove home like a mad person. I don't recall any lights, any cars on the road but mine. I pulled up into the driveway, barely stopping my car. By the time got in the door the hospital was on the telephone again. It was the doctor. He sounded so calm as he politely said, "Is this Mrs. Yarbrough?"

I said, "This is she." He continued, "We need you to get up to the hospital immediately. Kenny just expired." I was speechless and screamed silently. I turned around to my mother, who was a few feet away and calmly told her Kenny had died.

I heard screams, screams, and screams. Mine was silent. I stood there for a moment I couldn't believe it, not Kenny. I barely could breathe anymore. It didn't matter. Kenny had died and it was now my turn. I couldn't make it, wasn't trying to make. I began to wonder what I was going to do. The thought raced through my mind, Kenny's dead. Oh! God! I didn't think I was going to make it to the front door and to my car. I cried openly. I cried out, "Oh, Kenny, no! Please don't leave me." Not even realizing he was already dead. "My baby," I kept saying. Why? I was afraid for Kenny to die alone. I knew if there was a God he was there with him. But I felt I should have been there with him.

I walked out of the house feeling as though I had been hit by a tractor trailer.

I felt like I had felt six days ago—dead. I felt like I was a walking time bomb waiting to explode. Regardless of what I feeling right now I had to get to the hospital. I thought of what happened to Kenny. Was he afraid? Did he call my name? All kinds of things surfaced through my mind. Were the doctors gentle to him? Did someone care enough to hold his hand as I would have in his last minutes on this earth? I prayed to God they treated my child as if he was their own.

Chapter 6
The Day

My husband, my son and I left for the worse day of our lives to face my child who was dead and who had fought so hard to live. I had prayed and prayed Kenny would make it. I was angry because the doctor promised me if he made it through the first forty-eights hours he would be out of danger. So many things failed me. My faith was gone. What did I have to hold on to? I continued crying, in and out of shock, calling Kenny's name asking God why? I cried openly. There were no more silent screams; there were no more tears in the corners of my eyes. I wanted the world to know how bad I was hurting. I wanted to let go. I had to first take care of Kenny.

I headed to what I was so afraid of facing, my dead child. It was over for Kenny, but the beginning for me. I rode to the hospital in the front seat of the car laid back with tears streaming down my face. I was too hurt to scream aloud so I screamed silently. Tears and tears were rolling down my face. The thought of Kenny dying continued to flash across my mind. I couldn't believe Kenny was dead. I kept saying maybe the doctor made a mistake. Maybe they called the wrong person. That was what I wanted.

The ride to the hospital was quiet. My husband was smoking cigarette after cigarette. It was so quiet all I could hear was him blowing smoke out of his mouth. My youngest son, Julius, was so quiet, trying to be understanding and strong for me. He gently was rubbing my head. I knew he was as hurt and helpless as I was. I lay back like a rag doll. Finally we arrived at the hospital. My heart began to leave me, it was racing so fast, and I could barely breathe.

At this moment I knew I was going to die. I had to see Kenny first. We walked the long hallway to the critical care ward. For the first time it seemed longer than before. I wanted to go and I did not want to go. I knew Kenny was dead and a part of me said no, he was not. I did not know which one to believe. I was afraid to open the door to the critical care ward.

I had to wait to see for myself. I opened the door and died right before the nurses and doctors. They did not know. I passed out, only to wake up in a chair with ammonia under my nose. The doctor called my name three times. He said if I did not get myself together they couldn't allow me to see my son. I knew right then and there it was no longer about me. I had to see Kenny.

I pretended to be okay. I knew that was the only way I was going to be able to see Kenny. The doctor asked if I was okay and I think I said yeah. They escorted us over to where Kenny was this morning. This time the curtain was drawn closed. I opened the curtain and I screamed. "No, God, no!" I wrapped my arms around him for the first time in seven days. I had wanted to do that. I could not do it before as much as I wanted to because of the machines in the way. I climbed on the side of the bed and lay beside Kenny and cried and cried. I wanted to scream. Again, I thought about the other patients who were already in the critical care ward. They would have heard my screams and I didn't want them to think they, too, were going to die. I always thought about everybody but me. My child had died and yet I was caring about the other people in the ward. What about the people who killed Kenny? What were they doing now? I wanted to run off the ward screaming, but instead I screamed silently. I hugged Kenny and kissed him. I held on to him. I couldn't let go.

I did not want to go. My husband told me I had to leave. I was holding on to Kenny and could not let go. His body was still warm and I couldn't believe he was dead. I believed he knew I was still there, or that was what I wanted to believe. After all the tugging eventually my husband separated me from Kenny. A part of me stayed on the bed beside Kenny and a part of me walked away. At the thought of me never seeing or hearing his voice again I sat down on the floor and cried and cried. I felt I couldn't leave the hospital. This would be the last time I would see Kenny. When I saw him again he would be in a coffin. "No," I screamed. I couldn't leave. I held on to the bed with Kenny wrapped tightly in my arms. My husband and son helped me up and I continued looking back at Kenny. I couldn't leave him alone. I wanted to stay there with him. My heart was broken in a million pieces. I didn't want to go on. For once I thought about me.

I left the room where Kenny was lying dead on the bed and went down the long hallway I had traveled for seven days. Not intentionally I walked over to the window, and there I saw a hearse. I wanted to run back into the room so Kenny couldn't leave me. I began to cry because I knew it was there for Kenny. I wanted to jump out of the window and down into the hearse and wait for him. There were two people standing beside me, so helpless. I started to walk down the hall and again I passed out. This time when I came to I was in a lounge with family members. I did not want to be with them, I wanted Kenny. How long had I been out?

I begged my husband to let me go back once more to see Kenny, but he would not. He held me tightly wiping my face, and walked with me slowly down the hall, an all-to- familiar hall. A place I knew I never wanted to see again. A place associated with nothing but bad memories, pain, and sadness. A place that had become my home for days, and now I walked the hall alone, leaving behind the most important reason for the hallway; Kenny.

Talking about faith, and trust; I had none. I felt God had let Kenny die. I couldn't pray. The most important prayer was not answered. God, please don't let Kenny die. As many nights as I prayed Kenny still died. Talking about a loss of faith in God. I had none. Where was God? I asked over and over again.

My mom always says God is everywhere. Again I asked where was he when Kenny was shot. Where was he when Kenny died? Where was he?

I walked slowly over to the elevator; I was too tired to push the button. I stood there staring at the button and didn't want to push it. I didn't want to leave. Yet I had no reason to stay even though I wanted to. My husband wanted me to wait until he got the car. He was afraid to leave me. He thought I would go back into the room where Kenny was. I remember coming into the hospital, we had parked the car so fast I forgot where we parked. I didn't want to find the car. Finding the car meant leaving Kenny. I was not trying to do that

I felt trapped in my own body. I felt I wanted to stretch out on the floor and scream; instead I was heading toward the door. It felt as though the elevator ride was much longer. The elevator stopped. The door came open; so did my heart. I didn't want to get out. I stood there crying and thinking I couldn't leave Kenny alone. My son grabbed one hand and my husband grabbed the other. I felt like a rag doll. I felt as though my life ended in the hallway of the hospital. I could barely get in the car; it hurt to move. I got in and fell over to the other side, crying, so helpless. I remember leaving the hospital. I asked the doctor what they were going to do with Kenny's body. I wanted to know before I left. Yes, he was dead but he was still my son. The doctor informed me his body would be going to Baltimore for an autopsy. I screamed but silently. I didn't want him to go alone. If I could have I would have ridden with him, but I couldn't. So I left, feeling sadder that I ever had.

My husband and son got in and they both reached for me at the same time. I cried; it seemed to be forever. My body felt like 2000 pounds of lead. "Oh, God, why?" was all that I could say.

As he started up the car, I started to cry. I didn't want to leave the hospital. Leaving tonight meant I would never see Kenny anymore. I screamed but silently. The car began to move and I got dizzy from the motion. I tried unsuccessfully to raise my head. I couldn't move a muscle in my body. I felt like someone had torn my body apart. My heart felt as though it had been ripped out and cut in small pieces. If only I could tell you how I felt less that an hour after losing my son. I can't explain to you. Only God knows.

The ride home took much longer. No one spoke a word. My son was in the back, sitting behind me in the middle, rubbing my head. I was ever so thankful for him. I needed someone to touch me at some point to assure me I was living. I felt I was dying, slipping away slowly. His hand kept me awake. It kept me realizing I was alive. I felt hopeless.

It seemed as though we had been driving for hours. I knew we should have been somewhat close to the house. We were closer than I really wanted to be. I was home. A home I no longer wanted to go to. I wanted to jump out of the car and run and run and run. I could not stand still. I felt I had to move, do something. I was falling apart.

The car stopped and I knew we must have been home. I raised my head just a little to find out where we were. Yes, I was home and so was my family. How could I get out this car and face my family? My pain was too deep to be in the presence of anyone who knew me. They had to feel my pain; they had to see my pain. Why did I feel I had to hide it? I never understood why I felt I had to hide my pain.

I wanted to be strong, but I couldn't. As the door opened there stood my mother. I walked into her arms and buried my head into her chest and cried, "Oh, Mama, Kenny's dead. I can't take it. I can't go on."

She rubbed my head and said, Kenny wouldn't want you to do that. I didn't care; I wanted to die. She cried with me. She began reciting the 23rd Psalm as she always had. I couldn't relate to anything but Kenny was dead. One part of the 23rd Psalm says, "I walk through the valley of death; I will fear no evil." I felt a lot of evil.

I laid my head back on the chair and begin to cry again. I couldn't breathe. My mom told me to breathe in and out. I couldn't. There was no air to breathe in or out. I wanted to die. My lungs felt as though they were closing up on me. I gasped for air. I ran to the front door, only to make things worse. My chest began to hurt very badly. It felt as though I had been hit in the chest with a hammer. I grabbed my chest and sat down.

My brother Michael became very hysterical and yelled, "Dial 911." Anything in white was the last thing I wanted to see. I felt they were responsible for letting Kenny die. I had to blame someone. I begged my brother not to call but he somehow ignored me. I lay back hoping I would die. I no longer cared about breathing; I no longer realized my chest was hurting. All I knew was Kenny was dead.

The paramedics arrived and I wanted to scream. I didn't want them to touch me. He asked what caused my chest to hurt. I couldn't talk. My brother responded, "Man, she just lost her son." He wanted to take me to the hospital. I refused to go. I was feeling bad, but I couldn't go to the hospital. I couldn't trust them anymore. They left. I lay on the bed and cried myself to sleep. My mom stayed at the end of the bed. I wanted to wake up and I wanted to stay asleep; I wanted to die.

The telephone rang. I jumped up; my mom said it was not the hospital. I looked as though it might be. Within minutes I remembered Kenny was dead. I screamed again silently. I lay back on the bed. My heart was still hurting from the pain from the loss of my son, my best friend.

I was crying, asking God why; why was I being punished? What had I done wrong? Guilt was all over me. Guilt was nothing but the devil trying to kill me, and he was doing a good job. My faith was gone. I felt I had no one in the world who understood my pain, not even God.

The telephone would not stop ringing; I guess so many people cared about Kenny. I couldn't continue to hear the sound of the telephone ringing. I thought of all the times when it did ring and it was the hospital. I thought to myself, who is it now and what could anyone want? What could anyone do to make me feel better or to take away this horrible pain?

My body felt as though it had been cut and salt was being poured into the wound; you name it I felt it. No matter which way I moved it hurt, so I tried to lay still. I continued to cry, calling Kenny's name.

My mom never left my side. I dozed off to sleep around 10 p.m. When I woke up it was 1 a.m. I wondered how I slept through the pain ripping my body apart. I guess even though I was angry with God, he was watching over me. He gave me peace in the midst of the storm. And believe me, it was a storm! I felt as though I was flying, hitting air pocket after air pocket. I was so shook up but God never left me. It had to be him. Without him there was no way I could have made it through the night.

I was sitting on the side of bed thinking Kenny was shot on a Friday and died on a Friday. I began to hate Fridays. When Thursdays came I got depressed. It almost became a trend. More kids were dying on Fridays. I gathered because it was the end of the week, people got excited and didn't know what to do, so they went out on a shooting spree. It happens Friday after Friday. Children are dying and mothers are crying. It became an all-to-familiar scream, a scream that sounds like pain deep down in the pit of your stomach. A pain to hard to bear, a pain that is silent.

Friday in the real world meant the end of the week; you get to rest. Friday meant nothing to me but the remembrance of Kenny's death. I called it Black Friday, because you can't see through black and I couldn't see through the next minute or hour. I had no reason to look forward to Friday. The first Friday after Kenny died became harder and harder. I kept saying week after week, month after month, what was Kenny doing a month ago, meaning the last month he was here. It was hard for me to move on.

Chapter 7
The Day After

Saturday morning came and I had to get up. I tried to but I couldn't. I felt I had the weight of the world on my shoulders. I had to prepare for the nightmare of my life; Kenny's funeral. I repeatedly said to God, crying, "I can't do it." I had no idea on what I was supposed to do. Being a child of God and having a praying mother, God lead me and protected me. He shielded my broken heart.

I began to reminisce. I said, "Kenny was here last Saturday." I tried to remember what took place in my life last week. I remember I was at the hospital waiting in the lobby for visiting hours. Now what was I doing. Preparing for a funeral. I screamed silently. I called for an appointment to visit the funeral home. I didn't want to go. My choices in life were now limited. I had to go with the flow.

Chapter 8
Preparation for a Funeral

I was counting the days. It was now Sunday, a very sad day of the week. To experience the death of a child on a Sunday morning was even more devastating, especially listening to your favorite gospel station. I was angry with God and nothing made sense. The songs didn't coincide with the meaning. "He's Able." If he was able, then why did Kenny die? I turned the radio off and lay silently. I wanted Sunday to end but Monday not to come either.

Preparing for the funeral was so hard. I knew it had to be done and I had to do it. I wanted to cry, but what good would it have done. I waited as long as I could before going to buy him a suit. I went on Tuesday morning after I received a telephone call that Kenny's body was here from Baltimore. I went to the nearest store I could find. I didn't know what size to get him. Kenny loved to wear jeans and a t-shirt. I couldn't bury him in that because I wanted to see him as a young man for the last time. Him dressed in a suit was my dream. He was such a handsome young man and I knew if he hadn't died he would have been even more handsome. Right now I would give the world for him to walk through the door with baggy pants on. I wouldn't care.

I went to a store where they had the best suits. I've always wanted the best for him from the day he was born until the day he died. The young man who helped me knew Kenny which made it even harder for me. He tried not to show his emotions. He tried his best to take care of me as quickly as possible, and I thanked him for his patience and understanding. By the time I was ready to pay for the suit and tie I broke down in tears. I was so hurt Kenny was dead. I gave my brothers the money and ran out of the store and sat on the side of the curb and cried. I buried my face in my hands, trying to hide the flow of tears that was running down my face. Within minutes they came out of the store with the suit. With one hand Eugene reached down to help me up. I reached up and he put his hand around my head and I buried it in his chest and cried. I was so confused I did not know what to do. All I could do was cry.

At nineteen years of age Kenny still had some maturing to do. He had already gathered a little hair on his face. He thought he was grown but in my heart he was still my little boy. That little golden brown boy with big brown eyes and sandy-colored hair running through the house with an orange in his hand; the little boy who wore a brown cowboy outfit on Christmas morning; the little boy who had on a brown cowboy hat and the matching boots; the little boy who thought he was Superman and jumped off the pool table, landing on a coat hanger and had to have stitches on the right side of his eye. He was just a typical kid anyone could love. Those were my good memories.

Now all I had were sad memories, memories of my little golden boy. Memories that will be with me forever until the day I die. I knew if it would have been the other way around, Kenny would have had a lot of good memories of me. Instead I was preparing for a funeral.

The thought of what was in the bag and the reason caused me to scream silently. We walked to the car which was parked across from the store. I was okay coming to the store. Going back seemed as though it took forever. Eugene opened the car door, placed the bag behind me, and walked around to open his door. I couldn't reach over to open it, I was too weak. He shook his hand as though to say, don't worry about it. I wish I didn't have to.

Tony asked if I needed to get anything else. I couldn't talk. The most I could do was shake my head no. He drove out of the parking lot, heading back to where I had no desire to go; home. The ride was quick and quiet, which helped us. They knew there was nothing that could have been said which would have been comforting to me, so they did what was best; said nothing. I really appreciated it.

We pulled up in the front of the house; there was nowhere to park. They told me to get out in the front of the house while they tried to find a parking space. I reached for the bag in the back but my younger brother Eugene told me to go ahead, he would bring it. I didn't want to go in. I walked slowly toward the door. My mom opened the door and asked if I got the suit. I replied yes and kept walking. I guess she wanted to know where it was. I told her Tony and Eugene had the bag and they were parking the car. She said, "Oh" and asked if I was hungry. I could not eat yet. I sipped here and there, but as far as eating, I could not. I felt guilty. Kenny could not eat so why should I? I walked over to the nearest chair, sat down and closed my eyes, hoping this was just a bad dream. I could not believe Kenny was dead. In spite of me seeing him at the hospital I still could not believe he was gone. My heart hurt. I kept my eyes closed, pretending to be asleep, hoping no one would talk to me. My mom had questions but I did not want to talk to anyone. She would not leave me alone. Everyone else sort of drifted off from me except my mom.

As I lay still with my eyes shut, the telephone rang and my heart almost jumped out of my body. I immediately though it was the hospital. I had to calm down and remember Kenny was no longer there. I sat back and calmed my heart down. My heart was racing faster than ever. I grabbed my chest and thought I was going to die. It was hurting and I began to grasp for breath. I got up quickly and went to the front door to get air. That was what I was taught in the hospital when Kenny was shot. They showed me how to breathe in fresh air. The doctor also showed me how to breathe into a paper bag. It sounded strange, but it worked. If I could have put my head in and closed the bag I would have. I then thought who was going to bury Kenny? I had to put down the bag. Suicidal thoughts raced through my mind many times.

Monday meant me calling the funeral home. One day we all have to go there for a loved one. Why so young, why Kenny, and why me?

I did not deserve to be making funeral arrangements for a nineteen-year-old child who was healthier than you and me. I went to sleep dreading the moment I would have to wake up to in the morning. But somehow I had no choice.

Monday came and I did not want to get up. I lay in the bed scared to get up, scared to go to the funeral home. I cried and kept saying, "No, God, I can't go and do this, why me?" I got no answer so I lay there wondering how and where was I going to get the strength to get up and go to a funeral home. I never asked God to give me the strength to do anything since Kenny's death. I knew God understood my anger. I knew no matter what, he was going to see me through whether I wanted to or not.

I called the funeral home to make arrangements. The voice on the telephone was very soft but it did nothing for my broken heart. She asked me if they already had the body. I paused for a moment. I thought, you may have the body, but he is my child. It sounded as though he was now their property. I said, "Yes, you do." She asked for his name and I said, "Kenneth Smith. She politely said with no care in the world, "Oh yeah, his body came in today." I wanted to scream. Before I could scream she gave me an appointment for tomorrow, Tuesday at 3 p.m.

We arrived at the funeral home an hour before time. I wanted to get it over, whatever I had to do. The door came open and a little old lady came out. She asked me my name and who was the deceased. I was speechless, so my husband responded. I screamed at the thought of Kenny's name. She asked us to follow her. We did and we went into this office full of paper on the desk. I couldn't imagine how she could find anything on the desk. A body could have been under the paperwork and she may not have known.

There were two chairs in the office facing her. She asked us to have a seat. My husband pulled out one chair and then pulled out the other chair and sat down next to me. The first thing which came out of her mouth was, "Do you have an insurance policy?" I looked as though do you care about anything other than the money? I understood it was a business, but what about my child? He was already dead and they were going to get paid regardless. It was not like if I didn't pay them they would kill him, he was already dead. I became very agitated by the mannerism of this little old lady. She had lived her life, my life, and yours. Maybe that's the way you have to be in this business. You can't take everybody's sympathy and make it your own. I knew she saw many saddened faces every day, so she had grown accustomed to this. I put her unconcerned attitude behind me and did what I came to do, which was to make funeral arrangements for my child.

After signing our lives away we walked down this long, dark, dirty looking hallway to this storage like elevator. It looked as old as she did. She pushed the button and the door squeaked. It sounded as old as she did. Before we could go up the door came open. It was a dark hallway. We walked past two closed doors. The third door was open and filled with a row of caskets. I screamed silently as she talked. She said, "I'm going to leave you all to make a decision." I couldn't understand why she had to leave us in this creepy-looking place. I hurriedly picked a casket and within minutes I was back at the starting point, in her little office. She said, "Oh that was quick." She pulled out the paperwork we had started to fill out. It couldn't be completed until we picked out the casket. By the time she finished hitting the adding machine we were at $5,000. I signed the form sending the payment to them. That was the last thing I cared about. I stood up and she said, "I'm not finished," but I was. I had to get out of this place. I wanted to get out of there as fast as I could. I signed the papers and left. I pushed the button and went to the first floor and sat until she and my husband came down. Just as I sat I heard footsteps and it was them. She walked over to me to tell me to bring his clothes in by Wednesday. I nodded my head and walked away. I was too hurt. I couldn't take it anymore. I wanted to run away to where my life was not a disaster. I kind of slipped away from the little old lady in the funeral home. I knew I had to come back again to view the body. I didn't want to, but once again I had no choice. She gave me an appointment at three o'clock on Wednesday to bring his clothes.

As we were leaving, we passed another family sitting there waiting to do what we just did. My heart cried for them because I knew it was not going to be easy, so I prayed for them. I asked God to stand by them and give them the strength they needed. I never asked for strength for myself because I was too angry.

We had walked out of the funeral home hand in hand, almost like two lost children. We were devastated, but we held onto each other. I was hurting and so was he.

That was an ordeal I never wanted to experience again in my life. I wish that could be, but it wasn't. I had to walk this road again in May 1996. I lost my strength, my salvation, my mentor, my main reason for trying to live again, my shoulder I knew I could lean on, a voice that only spoke positive things to me no matter how hard I wanted to hear the bad things, she gave me nothing but a dream, my best friend, my MOM. I cried out loud for the first time. It was no longer a silent scream. It was real. I screamed silently for years to protect her, then she was gone and there were no more silent screams. I wanted the world to know the pain that had been inflicted upon me again.

Her only wish in life was for me to finish this book. I believe she felt this book would be my closure. She knew I was still holding on to Kenny. I couldn't let go. You know what it feels like to have real love, you just can't let go. You know the pain and the sadness love put you through yet you hold on anyway. That's the kind of love I had for her and Kenny, a selfish love. I thought they both belonged to me. I didn't want to share either of them with anyone.

As soon as I got home, I sat on the side of the bed in shock. I could not believe Kenny was dead. I knew I had seen the body. I just could not bring myself to believe Kenny was dead. Not Kenny. I closed my eyes for a second, hoping and praying this was just a bad dream.

I did not know what else it was going to take to make me believe it. I held on to my pillow, rocking back and forth on the end of the bed. The only words out of my mouth were "Dear God." I took in a deep breath and before I could exhale a tear rolled down my face. It was so strange, just one tear. What that was for I did not know.

I began to think, I have to do this and do that. I never once asked anyone to do anything for me. You would have thought Kenny was the only one left in the world. I thought so. I held on to a picture I had of him. He was never one who liked taking pictures. So if I found one you better believe I held on to it for life. I had to stand up. I felt I had no muscles in my body. I had to assure myself I was not dead. I felt at some point I was.

I walked back and forth to the end my bedroom, pacing the floor back and forth. I felt I was lost. Alone was not what I needed right now. All sort of things were going through my mind. I walked over to the window. I felt suicidal as I stared out and realized it was not worth the jump. It was not high enough. I would only sprain or break a foot and that would hurt. I didn't need any more pain. The thought on my mind was much more than a break. It was eternal.

With the thoughts of suicide racing through my mind, I knew I had to bury my child. I had to put my life on hold for just a little while. After realizing I could not die just yet, another reason came about why I could not commit suicide. I promised Kenny I would see to it that whoever was responsible for what they had done to him, I would be there to the end. I had to wait. I lost patience; I felt I needed to do it now. I could not so I sat down and stared in the mirror. I did not like what I saw. There was a very sad face with sunken red eyes with very pale skin staring at nothing. I did not know that person in the mirror. She was a stranger.

I tried to wipe away some of the sadness but I could not. I put down the pillow and walked to the door, and before I could open the door, my mom was coming in. I had to put on another face. I did not want to really hear what she was about to say. She had told me since Kenny's death God makes no mistakes. I could not relate and did not want to hear that. I know she meant well. It just was not what I wanted to hear.

I left the room feeling again as though the world was not on my side, not even God. I was too tired to fight anymore; again I was giving up as I did so many times before.

I opened the door and headed toward the steps, with my mother behind me. We walked downstairs almost as one. That's how close she was on my heels. I went over to the closest chair and she headed toward the kitchen. She had been trying to get me to eat. I couldn't no matter how hard I tried. I was sitting there when the telephone rang. It was the funeral home. The call was not a pleasant one since he informed me of the clothing he needed. It was always important what everyone needed but me. I needed Kenny. I wanted to scream.

Again who was I and what did I know? I knew one thing, I didn't want to go to the store, not so much for Kenny but because of the reason. I paused when he said I needed to bring underclothes. I said, "Why?" I then thought he needed to be warm, so why not? I asked the man if I could bring him some socks and he said it was not necessary. I wanted to so he said okay. I guess I was going crazy again. I felt I had been going crazy for a while now.

The time was winding down. I had to go to the precinct to talk to the police. I was afraid of what I might hear. I had spoken briefly with the detective on the case. He was very caring. He cared about Kenny. He had visited Kenny in the hospital. He said he was never aware of the extent of Kenny's injuries. He assured me he would do everything in his power to close the case. He was sure he was going to close the case and I was sure I had to close a casket. Forever. Burying a part of me.

While he was talking, I was screaming, but silently. He told me he had a suspect in custody. My heart dropped and I began to wonder who this person was. I thought I wanted to see him. I wondered how he could have shot someone and went home to eat and even sleep. I just couldn't understand. I needed answers and I knew the only answers would have to come from him, but I didn't want to talk to him.

I don't know why the detective told me he had Kenny's clothes in a bag. I never asked him. I screamed. I asked if I could have them, but he looked at me and said, "You don't want them." I looked startled. He said to me they had been cut off and were bloodied. I didn't care, I wanted them. He headed toward the locker where they were and I told him never mind. He said after the trial I could at least have his Timberland boots back. I would have liked to have my child instead of a bag of bloodied clothes, but that was all I could have for now and I was willing to settle for that.

Kenny had many female friends. He let all of them know his momma was the only woman in his life he loved. He told them all. He would go as far as telling them, "I don't care if no one loves me, my momma loves me." He had no shame in sharing that with his friends. I always smiled when he said that because I felt the same way.

On the way home I cried. I couldn't imagine life without him. I would close my eyes and I would for a moment, be in my own world... I could see Kenny so I never wanted to wake up. I laid my head back against the headrest, pretending to be asleep. I wasn't, I just couldn't talk. I was lost for words. I was lost in my own body. I cried silently, and openly.

It hurt, so I cried silently. It affected every part of my body from my head to my feet.

It didn't miss a part. When I cried my entire body hurt, it did its own thing. My chest would hurt; my eyes were burning from screaming silently. My head felt lighter than a feather, my feet were heavy, and they had to carry all the weight. I was no good; I felt as though I was dying. At least that was the way my silent screams left me.

I woke up after riding for fifteen minutes. I knew we should have been home or close to it, and close to it we were. There were cars parked on both sides of the street. I wanted to jump out of the car and run and run until I passed out. I ran but I was standing still.

The car stopped. I put one foot out of the door and there was my daughter, Starla, staring me in my face. She looked as lost as I did. I got out and wrapped my arms around her and walked slowly to the house. I could barely make it up the steps for people hugging me and kissing me. Some were anxious to tell me how nice of a person Kenny was. Some said how polite he was. Who knew better than me? I tried to steer him in the right directions, teach him how to be respectful. He knew what he had to do when he had to do it.

I managed to make it to the top of the steps. Looking through the glass door, more people were in the house. I wanted to scream and run the other way. I opened the door and went in. My mom was in my view and she noticed the sad look on my face and I saw it in her face.

We both were hurting. She was hurting because I was her daughter and I was hurting and so she hurt. She hurt because there was nothing she could do to ease my pain. She knew and I knew what I had to do. I wasn't about to pray. I was too angry. I hurt, I cried, I ran, I screamed, but I could not pray.

As I was walking toward the kitchen the telephone rang. My heart skipped a beat. Then I remembered it could no longer be the hospital. My sister yelled it was for me, but I had no care in the world to talk to anyone. Who could it have been who would have any interest to me? I walked over to the area where my sister was and took the telephone. I was hesitating, but I said hello. It was a heavy voice I knew but couldn't quite recognize who it was. Within seconds he identified himself as the detective handling Kenny's case. He had found the people who were responsible for Kenny's death. He wanted to at least let me know that. I thanked him but I knew it was not going to bring Kenny back. He said they were incarcerated in D.C., waiting to be expedited to Maryland. I felt like going to get them myself. I wanted to know what they looked like. Why that was important to me, I didn't know.

Nothing was a secret to my mom. She watched every move I made. She wanted to know who was on the telephone; I told her it was the detective handling Kenny's case. She wanted to know what was going on, and I told her they had found the people responsible for Kenny's death. She raised both of her hands and said loudly, "Thank you, Jesus!" Within minutes she was in tears, still praising God's holy name. She was a praying mother. She prayed for everything and everybody.

I stood there as my entire body felt lifeless. I felt like a statue. I felt like I was dead. I walked over to the closest chair and sat my tired, aching, lifeless body down. The room was filled with people, old and young, black and white; they all were all Kenny's friend. Everybody liked him. I believe if the people who killed Kenny had given him a chance, they would have liked him too. Knowing Kenny, he would never harm anyone. He was that kind of person. Again to know him was to love him.

Before I realized it Wednesday was here. That was the day I would get to see Kenny for the first time since his death. His body had been sent to Baltimore for an autopsy for the past two days.

I lay around all morning dreading the moment I had to go to the funeral home. I walked back and forth wondering was I going to do it. I wouldn't pray. How could I ask God to help me? He didn't help me when Kenny was dying. I couldn't find the strength so I cried silently. I lay across the bed. I closed my eyes and hoping to wake up to a bad dream. When I opened my eyes it was the truth, it was Wednesday and Kenny was dead and yes, I had to go to the funeral home.

I gathered the things they asked me to bring. I went into the bathroom, turned on the shower and let the water run and cried until I couldn't cry anymore. I was afraid and felt so helpless, wondering at the same time who would hear my cries. I felt I had to be strong for everyone else. I stepped into the shower for a moment and couldn't tell if the water was from my tears. They were running together. I wanted to stay in the shower forever so I could cry and no one would hear me.

I stepped out of the shower wet, with the weight of the world on me. I felt even heavier. I tried to dry my body, but the more I dried it the wetter it got from the tears, which would not stop. I couldn't take it anymore so I began to pray. I asked God to please help me. I dried off enough to leave the bathroom.

I opened the door and a draft of cold air hit my face. I wrapped the towel tighter around me and hurried into my bedroom. I barely shut the door before the telephone rang. I jumped and thought it might be the hospital. I had to remember Kenny was dead.

My mom thought she was the telephone operator, so she told me the telephone was for me. I walked over to pick up the telephone; it was my job. They were checking on me to make sure I was okay. I talked briefly and hung up. I had no strength to talk. The strength I had, I needed to go to the funeral home to view Kenny's body. The thought of me going to view his body caused me to scream but silently. My appointment was at three o'clock. I tried to stay busy,

73

but I couldn't find enough to keep me busy. After getting dressed, I laid across the bed. I stared at the ceiling and asked, God why me?

I knew I had to get up and walk around to let the blood flow through my body to do the impossible. I walked, I ran, I screamed but I could not go to view Kenny's body.

It was time to go. I stood up but my body stayed down. I didn't want to go alone. I was afraid. My husband and my two brothers, Tony and Eugene, accompanied me to the funeral home. They tried to talk but the sound of their voices made me cry silently. Everyone was hurting, yet I felt I was the only one.

The ride was no more than twenty or twenty-five minutes at the most. We seemed to have gotten there sooner than I wanted. Once we arrived at the funeral home I had to take a deep breath that I did not have. I knew what I had to do but whether I could do it was the question.

The car stopped and so did my heart. I could no longer breathe. I felt as though I was about to die. I was so scared at one point, was I going to have a heart attack before viewing Kenny's body? We headed toward the door. I felt like running back to the car, but I stayed.

The door came open and who did I see but the little old lady, I had seen two days ago. She still had that arrogant attitude. She asked for the clothes for him. I handed her the bag. I wanted to run behind her. I knew where she was going and I wanted to be there. I couldn't so I walked over to a chair and sat and cried silently. I had my family with me which helped a little. My heart felt as though it had been ripped out of my body.

We had been there for about twenty minutes. My husband and my brothers had gone outside to take a cigarette break. I sat waiting for the moment I could finally see Kenny. I heard a door open and thought it was the little old lady. Instead this time it was a tall, fairly thin man. He introduced himself as the mortician. I stared at him and was speechless. I heard another door come open and it was my husband and brothers coming in; they came back in just in time.

The man asked us to follow him. My brother took one hand and my husband took the other one and we walked together down the hall. This time not a word was muttered. By anyone. The door opened and so did my heart, I glanced over and there lay my child whom I had not seen for a week, and when I did he was in a coffin. I screamed for the first time but not silently. I stared at him and could not believe Kenny was dead. I glanced over and saw my brothers crying. My husband never showed any emotions so I felt he didn't care as much as I did.

I later found out the truth; he was trying to be strong for me. Being strong is okay, but being completely silent in a case like this made me wonder if he cared. I knew he cared and he always hid his emotions. When his mom died he didn't show any hurt at all.

The mortician asked me if everything was okay with the body? I screamed silently. I saw a couple of things. Kenny hand had ink on it, I guess where the police had taken his finger prints. He had little white particles in his hair. He asked me to wait out front until he did what I asked him to do. One thing about Kenny was his hands were always clean and he kept a hair cut. I walked back into the hallway still holding on to my brother and my husband hand crying uncontrollably. I didn't want that man to come back but he needed to so I could make sure Kenny's body was presentable.

Within minutes he was back. This time it wasn't as bad when he opened the door, my body was already in shock. I could never hurt as I did the first time. I looked over his body again everything was okay, but he was dead.

We left the funeral home headed to a home I no longer wanted to go to. I cried just thinking about Kenny. I wanted to scream. I couldn't. I felt trapped in my own body. I was now mentally scarred for the rest of my life. I felt lifeless, I had no care in the world, and I had no strength. For a moment I thought I had died.

I had to prepare myself for tonight, which would be the first time my family got to see Kenny. I couldn't imagine how they were going to take it. I knew how I felt. I went home scared to mention I saw Kenny. I knew I had to go home and regroup by 6:00 p.m. that was the time the wake was to be. I only had a few hours before returning to the painful place I had just left, the funeral home. It came quicker than I wanted it to. I screamed for hours and no one heard me.

75

I had the wake set up for the family a half-hour early. I wanted them to spend quite time with Kenny before the public came. I knew they were going to need that time. They loved Kenny and they were as devastated as I was. We all gathered in cars, cars, and cars we arrived at the funeral home. I was so scared for them and myself. I cried silently. They had no idea what they were about to encounter. We had not lost anyone close in the family. Kenny was our first death in the family other than my baby who died at birth.

The doors opened and there more screams from Kenny's friends who had arrived with the family. My family was still all over the place. I couldn't get them together. They had every reason to scream. Kenny loved each and every one of them. Kenny shouldn't have been killed. He had many cousins and many friends. Nineteen uncles, twenty-five aunts, seventy five cousins, two sets of grandparents, two children, two brothers, four sisters, a mother and a father, and two stepfathers. We all were hurting at some point, not physically but mentally. Kenny's death had a big impact on the entire family. I had to stand next to the casket, to keep people from knocking it over. I had not yet dealt with my family. How was I to handle it when his friends came? I dreaded the moment the door opened to the public. The funeral director had to call for an ambulance. My niece Lisa had become so hysterical she needed medical attention. I couldn't go out there to see how she was. I was going through a lot standing there. It was only fifteen minutes before the door open to the public. I was afraid. Kenny knew a lot of people, young and old.

I remember he had a crush on this particular girl. He would always come home and tell me how pretty she was. I always smiled when he talked about her. I wondered who she was and what she really looked like. The night of Kenny's wake this girl walked up to Kenny's casket and asked if she could kiss him. I looked at her and I knew this had to be the girl. She was pretty. She gently raised the veil draped over Kenny's casket and kissed him. I cried because I knew this was such a hard time for everyone including her. Many of my co-workers came to be by my side. I thank God for them. It let me know other people cared about me.

76

Kenny was to be buried on Thursday, which was tomorrow. I was in shock and walked around as Thursday was a long ways away. My house was full, and so was I. I was full of pain, sorrow and a broken heart. I felt there was no-one in the world who could ease my pain. Truthfully there was no one. That was why I cried silently. Nobody knew how bad I hut but God and me. He was the only one yet I couldn't cry out to him either. I had an angry pain. A pain that was so deep only God could have helped me. I wouldn't pray the anger kept me silent as my screams.

I wanted everyone to leave. I wanted to be alone, but they wouldn't go. I needed to think and I couldn't because there were too many people in and out of the house. People laughing, babies crying, the telephone ringing, the doors slamming; I was a nervous wreck. I wanted to scream forever. It was getting late and people were still coming in. I wandered if they knew what time it was.

I continued with the smile I had carried since Kenny's death. I felt I had to hide the pain. I never understood why I thought that. It was my child who was shot, it was my child who lay in the hospital for seven days hooked to every kind of machine, it was my child who died, yet I felt so secretly I had to hide the pain.

I walked the floor back and forth, afraid for tomorrow to come. Tomorrow meant the last day Kenny would be on this earth, the last day I would see him. I was scared yet I was too afraid to let anybody know. I walked to the front door and screamed silently. I ran but my feet never moved. I stared out the door at nothing and that was how I felt like nothing. Never in my life did I ever feel so lifeless was the day before Kenny's funeral. I knew that day meant the end and the beginning of a new life. A life I would have to try and live without my best friend and my son.

I went upstairs looking through my closet to find a dress to wear. To this day I can't remember where or how I got that black dress. I pulled it out of the closet and stared at it wondering at age thirty-five why I was preparing for a funeral. I should be at the peak of my life where I should have been doing more than preparing to bury a nineteen-year-old child. The thought of it made me cry. I walked into the closet, leaned on the clothes and cried. I was hurting. After crying for a while I sat on the side of the bed and shook my head and said, "Oh no, God why me?" Before I could get an answer I opened the door and ran to the bathroom, locked the door, sat on the floor and continued to cry.

I finally got up and looked in the mirror. I looked a mess. I looked like I had been in a fight and lost. My eyes were red and swollen, only the white part barely visible. I washed my face and went downstairs to see how many people had decided to leave. Quite a few had gone, but quite a few were still there. Mostly family and close friends stayed until at least 2 a.m. Those folks I left up. I walked over to tell my mom I was tired then went to bed. She hugged me and I went upstairs.

I walked toward the steps and I tried to lift my feet, but they were heavy. I grabbed the rail and walked as though I wore 500 lbs. I managed to get upstairs to my bedroom. All I could do was throw my body across the bed and cry. I didn't know what to do. My child was dead and who really cared. I felt I was the only one. Even though I knew Kenny was loved by many, it gave me no consolation.

I dozed off to sleep only to wake up to a body next to me. It was my husband. I didn't remember him even coming into the room. I wanted so bad to turn over and allow him to hug me, but I couldn't. I wanted no one to hug me. I wanted no one to love me. I wanted to die. Losing Kenny took away all the love I had. I felt I had no love for anyone, not even the man I married for the seven years, not even myself. I hated myself. I began to feel sorry for myself. I began to feel blamed for Kenny's death.

Chapter 9
Saying Goodbye

Morning came and it was the day. The day I was going to bury my son. I hurried into the shower so that I could cry alone. I never understood why I felt I had to cry silently. I should have allowed the world to know how bad I hurt, instead I cried silently. I got out of the shower and I felt like running down the stairs and out the front door forever. I felt my body had been overtaken by something. I walked into the bedroom with the weight of the world on my shoulder. It hurt to dry off, it hurt to sit down, and it hurt just to move any part of my body. I sat down and rocked back and forth, still holding my towel in my hand, crying asking God over and over again why? No answers, just tears.

I knew I had to get the children ready. I had the intentions but I couldn't do anything. I dried off and slipped into my housecoat, and walked to the kid's bedroom, only to find out they were being taken care of. I thank God for the help I got for the kids. For a week I didn't realize I had children. Not that I didn't love them, but I was physically, mentally devastated. My mind was lost. I barely knew at times who I was.

I got dressed and went downstairs, only to find a house full of people. I began to wonder if they went home last night. I walked by and I could feel the sadness surrounding the room. I saw the hurt on their faces and it made me cry. I walked into the kitchen where my mom was and that was where I stayed. I wanted to hide from the world. I stayed in there for at least twenty minutes. When I decided to come out of hiding my front room was completely filled. I could barely see my children for the bodies that filled my living room. I walked through the crowd toward the front door; it was more people, more cars. I wanted to turn around and run.

It was closer to the time. I was standing in the door when the hearse came around the corner. I backed up from the door and screamed silently. I didn't want them to come; I wanted them to stay away. Even though I knew they weren't I still hoped and prayed. I prayed this day will never come. As long as this day never came, that meant Kenny could stay here with me just a little longer.

Someone came in the house reminded me the hearse was out there. I pretended not to know. I looked and saw this big, tall man standing in the middle of the doorway with a book in his hand. He asked who was in charge. I looked as though I can't be in charge, because if I was in charge Kenny wouldn't have died. I politely said I was. He said we need to start lining up. My heart skipped a beat and I paused for a second to breathe again. Every breath of air in my body has been knocked out.

I looked for my husband and he wasn't around, so I called for him. He was upstairs getting dressed. He came down and I felt a little relief. I felt I needed someone. Kenny's father was there also. He walked over to me and grabbed my hand. I held on to his hand tight. He felt the pressure as I held his hand. He knew that meant I needed him.

The man began calling out the order of the list. The kids were sent out first to get in the family car. My mom and Kenny's father's mom got in the car behind the kids and everyone else followed. I walked as though I had all day. I knew I didn't have all day but it was the day, the last day I would ever see Kenny. I wanted this time to last forever.

Everyone got in his or her car. There was another funeral director outside his car, signaling cars to turn on their lights. I sat as motionless as ever. Staring, crying, afraid to bury my child. Knowing today would be the last day Kenny would be on this earth. Dear God, I can't do it. Why me?

Everyone turned on their lights; we left the home that now has no meaning. No true meaning. Kenny was gone and gone forever. The ride to the church was quiet. I looked back and saw lines and lines of cars. There were so many, we turned the corner and the cars coming for forever. I knew Kenny was well loved by so many. I closed my eyes, hoping that this was just a bad dream. We were getting closer to the church. We turned the corner and there sat a white hearse. I screamed. I knew that meant Kenny's body was in it. It was no longer a silent scream. I wanted to jump out of the car and get in the back of the hearse with him. All sorts of things were going through my mind. I felt I had done all I could, so what more could I do but die. I was ready, but God wasn't. He needed to use me a little while longer.

The funeral director got out of his car and opened the door to the car that carried my family. As we entered the church it was filled with friends of my husband, Kenny's, mine, his sisters and brothers, friends and friends. It was the sadness day of my life. I had nothing to hold on to.

Too many people lives depended on me, I had four children who depended on me and I depended on them to help me. My brother-in law performed the eulogy, Revered Larry Frazier. He was fantastic and eased a lot of pain for a lot of people at least for me. I thanked God for him every day. My sister-in-law Shirley sang Amazing Grace. My brother-in-law Tyrone sang "It's So Hard to Say Goodbye," and yes it was hard to say goodbye. I cried and cried through out the service, screaming silently. I was so close to the front I could have touched the casket; instead I stared in disbelief and cried. My body could no longer take it. I cried openly for the first time.

As they sang the piercing sounds of screams echoed the church. It made me cry more to hear my niece Tiffany scream and stump her feet and say, "Wake up, Kenny!" She repeatedly said, "Wake up." I wanted him to wake up too. She said, "I know you can do it Kenny, wake up." Tears rolled down my face faster than I could wipe them. It was very hard to close the casket. Closing the casket meant Kenny was gone forever to me. When they closed the casket I cried uncontrollably. I never cried since Kenny was shot, two weeks ago.

My body couldn't take it anymore of anything. I wanted to lie down in the church and close my eyes to the world. I couldn't give up just yet. I had to see to it that the people responsible for this crime were punished and I mean punished dearly. I felt I was being punished and I hadn't done anything.

We left the church and I screamed at the thought of leaving Kenny in the church all alone. Yes I sound crazy, but that was the way I felt, he was alone. The casket was being rolled in front of me. I wanted to stop the carrying of the casket. I didn't want Kenny to be put back in the hearse. Even though he was dead, I still needed him.

We drove to the cemetery and it was cold. I didn't want to get out of the car. I wanted to stay in there forever. Which meant Kenny would not be buried today. The thought disappeared as the director opened the door. I got out of the car and walked over to the opening where Kenny was to be laid forever. I cried.

We left the cemetery leaving my friend, my son in a cold place. A place where no one cared but me. The caretakers didn't care. They were only going to throw dirt over the casket when I was out of sight. I walked away without looking back and screamed silently. Even though it was a silent scream, this time for some apparent reason I felt someone heard me. I think that someone was God. He heard my silent screams for days and weeks.

The ride home was as quiet as the ride in. The look on my children's faces saddened me even more. Not only did I lose a son, they lost a big brother. A brother they had looked up to for the past nineteen years. I knew if I was hurting they had to be also. All I could do was bow my head in sadness.

I knew there was nothing I could have done to help fill the void they were feeling right now, because there was nothing no one could do for me. I think they were screaming silently too. I didn't now how we were going to make it. I didn't know what to do, what to say to the kids. I figured what would I want someone to say to me nothing and I didn't say anything. As I kept my head down I could feel they were watching me. At one time I did see my youngest daughter Starla staring, but she dropped her head quickly. I couldn't wait to get out of this car. I wanted never to ride in a limousine again. I hated the thought.

Within minutes we were turning into the neighborhood. The first thing I saw when turning the corner was Kenny's little red car, which he loved so much. That car broke down more than he drove it. He loved his little car. And I loved it because I know how much he loved it. The limousine stopped. I wanted to jump out and run and run until I couldn't run anymore. I wanted to scream, I wanted to do something, but I didn't want to go into the house.

People were laughing and talking. How, I couldn't understand. But again I could understand it wasn't their child who was murdered so they had no idea how I was feeling.

I became angry again, why me? Not that I wanted anyone to go through this, but I have thirteen sisters and brothers why me? Why not one of them? I felt ashamed saddened. I couldn't understand. I started blaming myself, asking myself, what did I do wrong? What could I have done to prevent Kenny's death? I couldn't find an answer, because there was not one and I was not at fault, and there was nothing I could have done differently. Kenny's life was in God's hand. I had no control and I knew that, so that was why I was angry with God. I knew Kenny's life was in his hand, yet he allowed Kenny to die. Why? He was only nineteen years old, just beginning his life. Not only I was angry with God for me, but also because Kenny has two children he would never see or hear the word daddy. And people say God is good. I couldn't see it. And that was what the devil wanted me to believe. The devil had control over my mind and was killing me slowly. There was no faith in my body. At least I thought there wasn't. God and the devil had control over my body. The devil was more in control because I was angry with God and I was feeling that way.

The devil was happy he had me. I did nothing to stop him. I was as bad as a drug addict even though I didn't do drugs. I was an alcoholic yet I didn't drink. I felt like I was just a no body, even though I had four children whom I love very much, more than anything in this world. My body was full of anger so that I sometimes scared myself. While everyone was eating I was pretending to be sleep. I wanted to disappear from the world. I loved them all in a special way. Each of them had a part of my heart.

One part of my heart had died and it was affecting the rest of my heart. I couldn't separate that part of my heart. No matter how hard I tried. Kenny's death affected my heart all over leaving that part of my heart hurting, too. I couldn't just tend to Kenny's part.

The house stayed full for at least another hour. I was tired and wanted to go to sleep. My mom tried to get me to eat. I couldn't eat if I wanted to, I was too weak. My body was lighter than a piece of cotton. I felt like the little flowers you pick off the tree. You know the ones we use to blow when were younger. I felt if you blew hard enough I would disappear. I kept my eyes closed and felt a hand covering my hand. I didn't want to open my eyes, but I did. It was Kenny's father kneeling in front of me. For a second I had to grasp for breath. They looked like they could be twins. They had the same features. Kenny was built and so was his father. He was letting me know he was leaving. He had driven here from Virginia Beach. I managed to get up and he gave me a hug. I needed that so bad I didn't want to let go. I felt we had Kenny together and what I was feeling he was feeling as well. I know he could feel my body shaking yet he embraced me even tighter. He whispered in my ear, I'm here for you. A tear fell from my eye.

I let go and he left. I sat down where I had been since I came home. I hugged his mother and sisters. I wanted to know when the rest of my family will be leaving. I needed to be alone. I needed to cry and I felt I needed to die. I couldn't take anymore. I was afraid to stand up and I felt I would pass out. I didn't want anyone to know how weak I was. Food was the last thing on my mind. Why couldn't I come back, eat, smile, and talk?

The kids were sitting at the table eating and my husband was talking to them. I was silent. I never understood that day. I remember eventually getting up. I walked to the front door; there was at least ten of Kenny's friend standing in the front of my house. It broke my heart and made me sad all over again. Whenever you saw Kenny's friends in the street, Kenny was always a step behind them or in the front or on the side. They all grew up together. They were neighborhood friends. If you saw one you saw them all. I didn't want them to see me, but somehow they did. I walked away quickly. I felt Kenny should be out there with them, not in a cold cemetery. He should have been alive.

Finally people were beginning to leave. I was a little happy I could now get up without people looking at me. I felt they were feeling sorry for me.

Chapter 10
The Beginning of a New Life

It was the beginning of a new life for me. I wasn't sure how to begin to live. I didn't care if I lived. For days and weeks I did nothing but cry. It was the hardest time in my life. I wanted nothing more than to end my life. It was and still is a pain which is embedded deep in my heart. To breathe sometimes it would hurt, even to think about Kenny dying it hurt. It's a hurt that will never go away. I ran and ran, and I screamed and screamed and no one heard me. I slept day in and day out. I slept thinking and hoping this was just a bad dream. I would hope to wake up and Kenny would be here. The hardest part is waking up to reality that Kenny was dead. I would go back to sleep. I wanted to sleep forever.

I couldn't go on. I tried and cried for weeks. I went back to work within a week hoping I could hide my pain at work, hoping to find peace. I couldn't; the pain, the hurt, the loneliness was there instead. I found myself sitting at my desk crying. I felt so helpless. I felt I had gone from a woman to a child in less than a month. My job was very considerate, and my boss told me if I needed to leave, don't come to her, just leave. She didn't understand my pain, but she had eight children of her own. She told me she could never imagine losing any of them. She said if anything happened to them she said she would die. I told her as nicely as I could not to say that because she might have to live up to those words. I always said that about my children. And I felt like I was going to die when Kenny died.

The first week back at work, I was sitting at my desk trying to work. And all I could think about was Kenny. I kept saying, "I can't believe Kenny is dead," even though I buried him two weeks ago. I still couldn't believe it. Not Kenny. I jumped up from my desk and got into my car and drove away. I wanted to drive and drive and drive to nowhere. I had no destination. I did just that. All I knew was I needed Kenny. He's been a part of my life for nineteen years. He's been my friend and my son for nineteen years. I kept asking myself, "What am I going to do?" I couldn't think anymore. I drove to the cemetery. I could barely see for the tears falling fast down my face. I cried out, asking God why? I continued driving and crying. I was not turning back. I was determined to go to the cemetery. I drove under the speed limit because I could barely see through my tears.

I drove into the cemetery. It was cold and dusty. The sun was beginning to go down. It was a very cold day and the wind was blowing so hard I could barely catch my breath. My tears began to freeze, but I continued to head toward Kenny's gravesite. I walked over to the gravesite and kneeled down on the cold ground and cried and screamed for the first time. I felt as though I wanted to begin digging up the gravesite and just for one more time hold him. I felt I needed to. As I was kneeling on the cold ground my tears were pouring down on me. I was getting colder but I couldn't leave. I needed to be by Kenny's side. I was tired of kneeling so I got up and sat on the side of another tombstone next to Kenny. Putting up a marker would make me feel Kenny was dead. I wasn't ready for that. When I do get Kenny marker I wanted a bench, where I could sit for as long as I wanted. I had to leave I wasn't ready. It was getting dark, and the cemetery closed at dark. I looked around. I was the only one visible. I didn't care. I didn't have a fear in the world. My only concern was Kenny. All I knew was I needed him. I walked away feeling I had no where to go, and told Kenny good-bye. I felt once again I had no home. I felt no one in the world understood my loneliness for Kenny. Everyone had his or her children but me. I felt I was being punished why me?

I walked over to my car feeling as though I was about to pass out. I barely made it. I leaned over my car and cried, asking God to take me too. I couldn't go on. I didn't know how. I had my cell phone in my pocket. I called my sister Jack, crying, asking her to take care of my children. She panicked and asked, "Where are you?" I wouldn't tell her. What could she do but tell me to come home? Where was home? I no longer had a home. I no longer had a life, I no longer had anything. She continued very hysterical, "Where are you?" I told her I am in the cemetery. She yelled, asking me why was I alone, knowing it was getting dark. She was going to send my brother Michael to come and get me. I said, "No, I don't want anyone to know where I am." My tears were drying as fast as they fell.

I pulled myself together enough to get into my car. I opened the car door and fell in the driver's seat, feeling like a rag doll. I laid my head back with tears rolling down my face, still with the cell phone in my hand. I could hear my sister calling my name. I pushed the button to end the call and drove out of the cemetery.

I pulled out into the street not even looking if there was a car coming. I no longer cared. All I knew was I wanted to be with Kenny. And if that meant me dying, then that meant just that. When I got home my mom told me if you ever want to see Kenny, you can't commit suicide. I didn't care, I was ready. I felt I couldn't wait on God for another five or ten years, I needed to go now little did I know God was in control. He knew I wasn't going anywhere. Yet I couldn't believe it. I felt as though I was going to die now. I wanted to go, but I knew I couldn't go anywhere. I had to see to it the person who did this paid for what they did to Kenny. I couldn't die just yet. I promised Kenny I would make sure this person was punished and punished dearly. I felt I was being punished, and I had not done anything.

I drove in the direction of home, but I didn't go. I parked in a grocery store parking lot and cried again. I couldn't go home and let my children see me this way. They always saw me as a strong person who could handle anything. I cried over and over again, saying to myself, "I can't go home yet." I lay back in the seat and closed my eyes wishing for the impossible, Kenny was not dead. I knew it was impossible, but I wished anyway. It was getting later and I had not seen my children. I sat up and looked in the mirror. I looked sad, and I felt sad. I started up the engine and pulled off. I drove slowly out of the parking lot thinking. What am I going to do when I get home? How am I going to explain to my children why my eyes are red and swollen? For once I cared about me.

I've cared about the kids and my family and how they felt. I loved them so much yet I was so distant. I wondered if I was afraid to love them and that was why I ran. I couldn't imagine what would happen to me again if another one of my children died. It would no longer be another silent scream. I want the entire world to know how bad it feels to lose a child. A child is a part of you. It's been attached to you for nine months. Depending on you and all of a sudden they're gone, it's devastating.

I pulled slowly into the driveway. Before I could turn off the car, a body appeared in the doorway. It was my youngest daughter Starla. She was probably worried about me. I know she loves me but I was afraid to love or have anyone love me. Love hurts especially when it's snatched away from you. You would think she had been sitting in the window, the door open so fast. I didn't have the time to wipe my eyes. I opened the car door and went into the house. Instead of sitting in the living room where the kids were I ran upstairs and locked myself in the bathroom.

At some point I felt I was living alone. I had no care in the world about anything, not even myself.

Three weeks had passed and I still believed Kenny was here. I kept telling myself he was just outside with his friends and would be home shortly. I think that was why I found it hard to accept his death. Mentally I had been waiting for Kenny to come home. Believing is seeing. I knew I didn't see Kenny yet I couldn't believe he was dead. How was I to go on? Why should I have to go on without him in my life? I cried for a moment and now forever. I have found a way to live, only through Christ. I knew of no other way to live. The only way to live is through Christ, he is the one.

While the children slept, I was awake watching over them. Being afraid of losing another child stayed with me for weeks, months, and years. I did whatever was necessary for their safety. I walked back and forth checking in their rooms. I don't know what I was afraid of; they were in their beds, sleeping soundly. Many times they never knew I was there. A many of nights, I cried as I stood watching over them. I couldn't imagine life without any of them.

I needed them now more than ever. They were my reason for holding on. I was barely holding on. I wanted so many times to let go.

Every day, for at least a month, there was a family member over at my house. I didn't really want any company, but I guess they didn't care. They stayed longer than I wanted them too. My sister Jack, especially. Everyday I would look up and she would be coming through the door. She would sit in one spot all day, only getting up to go the bathroom. Each time she got up I was hoping she was leaving, but she sat back down. We were always close. I knew if no one was there she would be. We both were pregnant at the same time. Kenny was born February 6, and her daughter, Freda, was born February 15. Freda and Kenny were very close from the beginning to the end. She missed him so much she had her license plate that said MSUKEN. People would look at her tag and try to pronounce it. It's simple: Miss U Kenny. I cried every time I saw her tags. I wanted the same thing on my tag, but we both lived in Virginia and two people couldn't have the same tag.

I tried for days, weeks and months to hide the pain. The more I tried to hide it the harder it got. Sometimes I grieved so hard my chest would be burning, feeling as though someone had stuck a torch to my body. The pain was not only burning it was killing me slowly. I never shared with anyone how bad it hurt. I felt they would never understand. And neither could I.

My mom stayed with me as long as she could. She had to go back home. She didn't rush because she knew I needed her and God knew I needed her. I was too afraid to share my pain with anyone else and she was my best friend, my strength, and my salvation. She kept me holding on. She recited the Twenty Third Psalms so much I would be hearing it in my sleep. I guess that's what she wanted me to believe in.

Time was slipping fast. I was sitting in the living room with my mom and sisters and the telephone rang, I jumped, and I forgot it couldn't be the hospital. Who could it be? My mom answered the telephone and it was for me. I walked slowly to the kitchen to get the telephone. My body was so heavy and I was so tired. Tired of pretending everything was okay. When I got to the telephone I could barely say hello!

The voice on the telephone was a male, a voice I recognized. It was the detective who was handling the case. He told me the people they thought murdered Kenny would be expedited to a Maryland facility on Monday. I was relieved to know they were locked up and could not hurt another child, another mother, another sister, another brother. I was ever so thankful, not for me but for the next family, knowing there was not going to be another family that would be hurting. He said as soon as the defendant had been returned to Maryland he would call me. I thanked him for being so caring and so helpful. He helped make my life a little easier.

Kenny's best friend was murdered last year and they never found out who killed him. I couldn't imagine how his mother felt; knowing someone murdered her son and one had been punished for it. I knew she needed some closure to his murder. Not that catching them made the pain go away, but it was a relief to know someone was at fault and would be punished. I knew punishing them would not bring Kenny back, but it would keep them off the streets.

Months had gone by and my family began to drift away, going back to their usual lives while I sat alone trying to find a life. A new life without my son, my best friend. It was hard. I though I was ready to live. I found myself crying and wanting to end my life.

I couldn't tell anyone about the hurt, the pain, the loneliness. I would get in my car and drive and drive. I found myself on at least two occasions at the scene where Kenny was shot. I had to go there. I needed to know where my child was at the time he was murdered. I wanted to stand in the spot where he lay, but I couldn't get out of the car. I sat and stared at the sidewalk where he lost his life. I cried at the thought of how cold it was on that day. It was very cold. Thinking about Kenny lying on the cold ground made me cry even harder. I wondered if he was thinking about me. I remembered watching this movie Robot Cop. When he was shot, he was on the operating table thinking about his wife and daughter. I wondered and I knew if Kenny could do that he would have been thinking about me and his son.

I've heard another story from a drug enforcement officer; he was shot at least five times. He said he was thinking about his wife and his two-year-old daughter. He said he was wondering if he would ever see them again, it must be true. I felt Kenny was thinking about me. A smile came across my face. The pain was still there, but for a moment I found a muscle that would allow me to smile.

I never let anyone know that I had visited the scene where Kenny was shot. I had to keep that a secret. I thought if I told them they would think I was crazy. I needed closure. I did what was best for me. I know I may have looked a little suspicious for a while, sitting there staring at the ground. I sat there for a minute and left. I drove up the street where the fire station was. I sat there and stared at the firemen. They were the first on the scene to help Kenny. He was not alone for long. That helped ease my pain, and I thanked God for those small things that kept me going.

I had returned to work, but it wasn't working out. I spent eighty percent of my time thinking about Kenny. I couldn't concentrate on my work. It was hard. I was tired of pretending, it was killing me.

Chapter 11
Grief

One day at work I began having chest pains. I didn't think anything of it. I went home and lay down, hoping they would go away. Instead they got worst. My left arm was numb with a sharp pain going through my fingers. It was hurting, I didn't care, and I lay there. I began experiencing shortness of breath. I then realized I needed to do something about it. I didn't want to go to the hospital. I had no trust in the doctors. I felt they let Kenny die; they might do the same for me. If I was going to die I wanted to die alone, not with someone standing over me, watching me dying and couldn't help me. I was angry. I called my mom and told her how I was feeling. Why did I do that? She began to tell me I needed to recite the 23rd Psalms and believe God was not going to let anything happen to me. Now how could I believe God was not going to let me die? I felt if God had control over all things why did he let Kenny die? I had no trust in no one other than my mother.

I waited for the children to come home before I went to the hospital. I waited for each of them to come in. Mentally I felt I wasn't going to make it. I at least wanted to see my children for the last time. After every one got in, I went to the hospital. I went alone. I didn't want anyone to go with me. I grabbed my purse and left. Before I could get out of the door, my youngest daughter, Starla, wanted to know where I was going. I couldn't tell her the truth and I couldn't lie to her. I told her I'll be back. I felt so bad leaving her. I glanced back and she was standing in the door, sucking her finger. I cried silently but I had to go.

The hospital was only five minutes from me. I thought if I had a heart attack at least I would be able to get my car into the driveway of the emergency room before dying. By the time I got to the hospital, I was feeling worse. I parked my car, but I didn't feel like walking across the street. It was so close yet so far.

I walked into the emergency room; I started to turn around because it was too crowded. There was barely a seat. I was really scared more than anything. Even though I had to sit beside more than one person, I didn't care, I was feeling too bad. I signed my name on the book. I headed toward a seat, but before I could sit they called my name. I turned around and walked over to the registration desk.

The nurse asked why was I there. For a moment I thought I didn't sign in. I remembered writing why I came. I came in for chest pains. She asked if they were sharp or dull. I told her I didn't know my chest just hurt. She asked if I was experiencing any pain in my arm and I told her yes. I wondered how she knew that. She then asked if I was experiencing any shortness of breath and I said yes. Maybe she was a psychiatrist. After taking my temperature she took me straight to the back. I remember hearing a woman say, "How did she just come here and is being seen already?" The nurse and I kept walking. I thought for a second if you only knew why I was here. I didn't want to be here, I didn't want to be first. All I wanted was Kenny, not to be dead. That was what I wanted.

There was a sign posted that emergency patients will be seen first. Because she didn't know she complained. She could have taken my place and my pain. I would have allowed her to. She couldn't imagine how I felt because Kenny wasn't her child and maybe she had never lost a child and neither did she know I had.

I walked into the back where the beds were. Some curtains were open and some were closed. The ones open were okay. The one closed made me reminisce. I immediately thought about when I went over to the hospital when Kenny died, the curtains were drawn. I screamed silently. I had no trust in the white coat people. They lied they told you what they wanted to tell you. They sure lied to me about Kenny's condition. If I hadn't felt so bad I would have left.

The nurse told me to get undressed from the top up. I tried hard but I couldn't. Another nurse came in and asked why I was here. I had just told the other nurse. I wondered if she wrote it in the chart and if she did, why was this nurse standing here asking me again. I took a deep breath and began to tell her I was experiencing chest pains. She asked the same questions the other nurse asked. Any pain radiating down your arm? I looked like please don't ask me if I am having shortness of breath but she did. I said, "Yeah." She wanted to know what I thought caused the chest pains. I sighed for a moment. A lump grew in the middle of my throat and I couldn't talk so instead I cried. She waited for a moment. I waited continuing crying. I began to tell her the reason for my being there. I couldn't tell her too much, it was too hard, too much to repeat. I hoped she was going to tell the doctor. If I had repeated this one more time I would die.

The nurse came back and told me the doctor requested an EKG. I thought how could he order anything when he hadn't been in to see me? I was glad to know I didn't have to answer any more questions as to why I was here. I heard a loud noise but I only saw a pair of feet. I wondered who it was. It was the technician to do the EKG. She was very pleasant and asked no questions, which made it much better. She was finished within minutes. As soon as she left no more than three minutes later here came not one but two doctors. I began to wonder what they saw. Was I going to die? It didn't really matter at this point. Kenny was dead. Whatever they found what could I do about it? I lay there and continued crying. I wasn't afraid of dying. I didn't want to do it myself. I knew suicide was a sin. My mom had already told me if I killed myself I would never get to see Kenny. I thought about it.

The thought of what my mom had been telling me stayed in my mind. I would see Kenny again. I remembered how long it had been since John Kennedy's death and I knew his kids were waiting to see him. I didn't have that kind of time. I couldn't wait another ten or twenty years. I needed to see Kenny now. I had to make up my mind to live or die. It wasn't an in-between thing. I couldn't make that decision even though I was in a position; my life was in God's hands.

The doctors were standing, there and yes, they asked that question anyway. "What brings you in here tonight?" The knot was still there. It had gone down a little. Hearing that question again it got bigger; almost choking me for air. I tried to talk between the knot being there and my tears, but I didn't know how they were going to understand me. They stood there patiently pretending to be reading the EKG report. I began to talk and they stopped reading. I told them my son was murdered and I didn't want to live. He said, "Looking at this report, you are not far from your wish." He asked how old I was, I said, "Thirty five."

He said to me, "With the amount of stress on your heart right now, it's a wonder you're living." I hunched my shoulders as though I knew and didn't care. He said they needed to keep me for a few days. I couldn't answer so I cried. He asked who was out in the waiting room with me. I told him no one. I had come alone. I went alone because I didn't want to let my children know how bad I was hurting. I felt I had to be strong for them as I always had been. If I needed to call someone there was a telephone. I didn't want to stay. All I could think about was that they let Kenny die. How could I trust anyone?

I remembered the promise I had made to Kenny, that I would see to it the person who did this to him would be punished. No matter what, I had to keep that promise.

I called home and my daughter answered the telephone. She wanted to know where I was. I couldn't lie, so I told her I was at the hospital. She became hysterical and began to cry. She asked me if I was going to die like Kenny. I cried even more to think my six-year-old would ask me something like that. She handed the telephone to her father. He asked where I was. I said I was at the hospital and they wanted to admit me. He got upset and and said, "No! I'll be there." He rushed over in less than fifteen minutes. I wondered what was going through his mind. Am I going to lose my wife now?

He came in the room and he and the doctors shook hands. The first question out of my husband's mouth was, "Why does she have to stay?" Very sadly he said, "Can I take her home and take care of her?"

The doctor immediately said no. "If you take her out of here she could go into cardiac arrest with the amount of stress on her heart right now. Now if you take her out of the hospital, I need you to sign papers releasing the hospital from all responsibility."

I took his hand and told him I would stay. I would be all right. I began to cry. I knew if I didn't calm down I would have an anxiety attack so I calmed down. As I was lying in the bed, I thought about Kenny, lying there for seven days and never waking up.

The children were home alone so my husband left, I stayed in the emergency room for the next six hours waiting on a bed. Again I was alone. My husband left to go home. He was upset I had left him and the children at home, so I told him I was sorry. He felt I shouldn't have been laying up in a hospital bed, while they were at home waiting on me. I wasn't in the hospital because I wanted to be. I was there because I had no choice. After losing a child you feel as though you have no choices.

I was where I didn't want to be. I didn't want to be at home either. I didn't know what I wanted. After finishing the paperwork for admission, my husband left. Again I was feeling alone. I lay there staring at the ceiling, thinking about Kenny, thinking about how if I was going to make it and how could I be a mother to my children and a wife to my husband? It was truly a concern to me. I loved my children and I loved my husband, but I no longer loved myself. I was hurting too bad. I began to cry again.

This time it was different. I felt the presence of someone. Someone I never knew before. I was lying in the bed, when someone said to me, "Take my hand." Instead I folded my arms and continued to cry. Whoever it was, whatever it was, the voice said again, "Take my hand." I continued crying with my hands folded crying, "No!" I didn't understand who or what it was. I was not giving my hand to anyone. For a moment I thought it was God wanting me to reach out to him. I cried even more, thinking God wanted me to trust in him after he let Kenny die. I couldn't imagine me trusting him. I held my hands tighter once I realized it was God. I couldn't do it. The tears started to flow even harder. I was scared.

I lay there for another ten minutes crying my life away. Whoever this person was they never left, they stayed there. I continued lying in the bed with my hands folded. Again the voice said, "Reach out and take my hand."

I gave in. I unfolded my hands and stretched out my hand. Unless you've come in contact with God you will never understand.

Within minutes after this episode for a moment my life became peaceful and quiet, so quiet it scared me. I had been through a storm. I dozed off and slept like I had never slept before. The noise of the nurse coming in woke me up. I woke up with a tear in the corner of my eye. The only words that came out of my mouth were, "Oh! Kenny. I miss you so much," and I began to cry again.

They rolled me out of the emergency room to my room. I was hoping to be alone. I don't think that was what the doctor ordered. Entering my room there was already someone there. They drew the curtains to slide me off the stretcher. Before I realized it I was lying next to a stranger. I didn't care and began crying openly. I was sad I was in the hospital. I didn't want to be there. I was hooked up to a heart monitor. Every time I moved it sent a signal to the machine. I didn't want to be hooked up to a machine. I didn't want to be confined.

I thought about Kenny being hooked up on the machines and I wanted to go home. I turned over and began to cry. I was looking down at the floor and saw a pair of shoes.

I didn't care; I continued what I had been doing for the past three months crying. A voice said Mrs. Yarbrough, I never looked up. I felt the bed go down as though someone had sat down. I raised my head just enough to see who it was. It was a doctor; at least I gathered he was a doctor, dressed in white. I wanted to scream. A person in white was the last person I wanted to be near.

He introduced himself. He was a psychiatrist. I thought now what. Are they now thinking I'm crazy? "What brought you here tonight?" How many people had asked me that question? How many people had I told the answer to? Too many! By now everybody in Greater Southeast Community Hospital knew why I was here. I thought about telling him I wanted to have it posted on the board why I was here. We talked for twenty-five minutes. He asked me the same question, but in a different way. He asked me what happen to my son and how did he get shot. I began to tell him, but before I could finish I was in tears, real tears, streaming down my face. I couldn't scream silently anymore. The silent screams were killing me.

He asked me how old was Kenny and in between the cries I told him he was nineteen. He shook his head and said, "Oh, he was a young man."

I said, "Yes he was." He wanted to know if they caught the people responsible for what happened to him. I again replied yes. In the back of my mind catching them would not serve any justice. It wouldn't make my life any better. He asked how was I feeling and I said, "You really don't want to know." He said that's why he was here for the truth. I said, "I want to die. I don't know how to go on."

He said, "You have every right to live."

I didn't think so and neither did he. I wanted to ask him if he had ever lost a child. If not he didn't understand why I wanted to die. He suggested I stay for a couple of days to get some rest and some professional help. Professional help was not going to help me. I needed God, yet I was not going to call on him. In spite of me not calling on him, I know he never left me. I knew in my heart it was nobody but God who brought me through. After the doctor left, I turned on my side and began crying like a baby, this time so loud the lady next to me asked me if I was okay. How could I be okay? When my child was murdered so senselessly. I knew Kenny wasn't ready to die. No matter what people told me, I knew Kenny was not ready to leave me. He loved me. She asked if she could get me anything and I said, "No thanks," then put the cover over my head as though that was going to stop the sound of my cries. I cried myself to sleep.

The next morning I got up and called home to check on the children. I knew they had to get ready for school without me. I felt bad but what could I do. I talked to each one of them and told them

I loved them. I talked to my youngest daughter who was six. She started crying. She said she couldn't go to school. I asked her why and she said, "Because you are going to die like Kenny." I promised her I wouldn't die. I told her I loved and I would see her when she came home from school. I had to keep that promise, I felt needed again at least for that moment.

I hung up the telephone, hurting all over again. This time a different hurt. A hurt I could fix. Kenny's hurt I couldn't fix. I lay there asking what must I do. I thought about it over and over again. I didn't belong here. I called the nurses station. She came down. I told her I needed to be discharged. She said she would have to call the admitting doctor. I didn't care who she called for me to leave. My children were hurting and they needed me. I needed them. She left and then two hours had passed with no nurse. I turned over again to push the button. I asked if anyone had time to talk to the doctor. She said no, they were waiting on a telephone call from the doctor. I unhooked my monitor and walked over to the bathroom. It went off sending a loud sound to the front desk. The nurse was there within minutes. She asked if I was okay and said I unhooked the monitor. I went into the bathroom, showered and lay back on the bed. I got dressed I was going home no matter what. I dozed off for a second and the next thing I knew there was a nurse standing there with a clipboard in her hand. She said, "The doctor said its okay for you to go." I thanked her, signed my name, and headed home to a life I was so afraid of. I buried a nineteen-year-old child less than three months ago. My life had been devastating, frustrating and humiliating. I asked myself so many times what must I do? I wish I knew.

I wanted to be the mother my children once knew. I knew I could never be that person again, but I was going to try to be the best of what was left of me. That evening when they got home we sat around the table and talked as usual never about Kenny. I felt they were hiding their pain. I knew it needed to be dealt with. I didn't know how, but I knew there had to be a way. I knew God was watching over me.

I called their pediatrician to get an appointment. They needed help. Help that I could not give them. I got the nurse on the telephone. I explained to her I needed to make four appointments for my children. I told her my son had been murdered and that my children were grieving silently, and they wouldn't open up to me. She gave me an appointment the next day. I was afraid. I didn't know what to expect, how were they going to talk to a stranger?

I told them I had made an appointment to talk to someone about how they were feeling about Kenny's death. They said they didn't want to talk to anyone. This time I understood yet I had to do something. I told them let's try anyway. My son was very reluctant to talk. He said, "Why talk to her? Did her son die?" I told him, I didn't know. He wasn't ready; he was angry.

We went to the doctor's office. I had to fill out four sets of forms. While filling out the forms they were talking to each other. I tried to hear what they were talking about. I finished the paper work and handed it to the receptionist. She took the paper work to the back. She called each one of them by their name. Normally when it's more than two children, they call you by your last name. They laughed. I was glad to see them smile for once.

While in the back I told them not to be afraid to tell the doctor how they felt. My daughter Julia said, "I don't want to talk to her." I tried to tell her it was for the best they talk to someone. She got angry and wanted to know why they had to. I begged her to tell the doctor what she was feeling.

The door came open and they all looked up, then looked at each other sadly; as though what am I going to say? The doctor introduced herself. She started by saying, "Who's the oldest?" Of course Shundra raised her hand. She said, "Who's next to the oldest?" Julius and Julia raised their hands. She said, "How can both of you be next to the oldest?"

They said, "We're twins."

She said, "Okay, who's the oldest twin?"

Julius said, "I am by ten minutes."

She looked at Starla and said, "I guess you are the youngest." Starla nodded her head yes. I thanked God for them.

She asked, "Who wants to be the first one to tell me why you're here?" The room got so quiet you would have thought it was empty. I looked at them picking at their hands. They begin to cry. Shundra spoke up choking out the words she missed her big brother and she couldn't understand why someone would kill him. The doctor handed her a tissue. I held back the tears. Julius spoke, saying he couldn't understand either why they killed his brother. He was a little stronger. He fought back his tears. Within minutes they all were crying, including me.

The doctor knew how hurt we all were. She ended the session by saying, "I will see you all next week." They sat quietly as I made their next appointment. After getting on the elevator they said, they did not want to come back. I understood why they couldn't and wouldn't want to come back. It was hard to talk about such a loving brother and son who died so violently.

We stopped by McDonald's to get something to eat. I was sitting there physically but mentally I was somewhere else. While sitting there who came through the door but one of Kenny's friends. He walked over and hugged me. I wanted to scream. Wherever you saw one, you saw the other, this time I saw him alone. I screamed silently.

The kids finished eating and we left. I took them home. I went upstairs to sit on the side of the bed. I tried to talk to my husband. I told him he should have gone with us. He wouldn't talk about Kenny either. If and when he talked about Kenny he was under the influence of alcohol. That was when I found it to be the hardest time to talk to him.

While sitting on the side of the bed, the telephone rang. There were times I would still jump. I jumped up when they called my name. I knew it was no longer the hospital. It was the police officer. He called to let me know the person who murdered Kenny was going to be arraigned next week. All I could think about was I would now get to see the person who shot and killed my son. My best friend. His children will never get to see him. They often ask me why their father died. Sometimes I would have an answer for them and sometimes I wouldn't, and sometimes I couldn't.

Chapter 12
Survival

Surviving a new life, and that was what it was a new life. A life I've never lived before. A life so full of pain, loneliness, and sadness. A path I've never walked before. A scary path, a narrow path. A path I never wanted to walk through again. A part of me knew God was with me and part of me felt I was alone. When I woke up I hurt, and I think when I was asleep I hurt. There seemed to be nothing in my life but pain and sorrow. The days were long and the nights were short. I walked back and forth in the midnight hour, feeling as helpless as ever. It seemed to get harder when night fell. I felt lonely, and sad. I guess because everyone was asleep, and I had time for me. Time to grieve. A time I had so little of. It was very frightening. I was afraid for my mind to be able to be opened to believe Kenny was dead. I kept saying to myself, "He's not gone." I would walk through the house rubbing my hand through my hair, crying and telling myself Kenny was dead. I kept saying to myself, "He's not gone." I couldn't believe Kenny was dead. I felt I was losing my mind. I asked God why over and over again. I got no answer.

Instead of sleeping, I was reminiscing over my best Christmas of 1989. It was a beautiful year. It wasn't snowing, yet it was beautiful. It was cold, the trees swaying just enough to see the leaves moving and to feel a breeze. Kenny and I were happy. I was sitting on the end of the chair when he walked through the door. He was so happy. Yet within three days, I had no idea he would be gunned down. Earlier in

PATRICIA A. YARBROUGH

the week, he had been running around getting ready for Christmas, buying gifts for his sisters and brothers. He asked me what I wanted for Christmas. I told him what I wanted he couldn't afford. He asked, "What is it?" I had always wanted a computer. He left and I continued doing my housework.

He came back later with a bag. He said, "Here's your Christmas Present." I asked what was it. He said, "Open the bag." I don't like surprises. I opened the bag and pulled out a box. I was taking my time, he was anxious. I opened and closed the box twice. I then opened it. I peeked in the box a little. I looked twice. I then decided to open it. I looked at him and he said, "Ma, come on!" I finally opened it; it was a beautiful gold watch with diamonds around the face, very petite and dainty, like a bracelet watch. He even put it on.

I said, "No, Kenny. It's only Christmas Eve." He said, "Remember what you always told us; you don't know if you will be here for Christmas." I kept it on for about an hour. It was gorgeous. I loved it. That was the last time I had a merry Christmas. Kenny was shot four days later.

That's when I experienced the real beginning of a new life. A life without Kenny. A life I know longer wanted to live. A life which had no meaning.

I looked at my life in 1990; it was disaster. There were times I didn't know if I was coming or going. There were times I didn't how to do nothing but cry. There were times I would go places and not know how I got there. There were times when I would see a person who reminded me of Kenny, and I would stare, knowing it was not Kenny. There were times and still there are times when I don't believe Kenny is dead. I walked around with my head lighter than a feather. My feet had to carry my body and there were times my feet didn't know what to do but carry me in circles.

My first Mother's Day was horrible. I tried to sleep all day, but instead I was awakened by the smell of fresh roses, and the rattling of paper. My children had gone out and brought me a gift and flowers. I got up and ran out the house. I felt bad, afraid, and helpless. I had a void in my life that could absorb the world. I apologized to my children. I wanted to be there for them. I couldn't as hard as I tried.

I had no strength Kenny was not here, he was gone, and gone forever. That thought stayed in my mind; Kenny was gone. I screamed silently.

I felt I was no longer a mother. I drove to the cemetery crying my heart away. I thought about Mother's Day 1989. We had all gone out for breakfast, Kenny left out as soon as we placed our order. When he got up, I asked him where he was going. He said, "Ma, I'll be back." I didn't care; at least I knew he was coming back. Within minutes he walked back through the door. I didn't see him when he actually came in the door. I must have been doing something. I looked up and he had this big smile on his face. I asked, "What have you done?" He said, "Nothing," so I continued doing what I was doing.

We waited for another fifteen minutes for our food. He ordered so much food. While we were eating I saw everyone looking at the front of the store. I turned around and the waitress walked over to me carrying a dozen of long stem roses. She said, "Happy Mother's Day." I cried and smiled. I got up and hugged him. That's where he went when I asked him where he was going. There was a florist across the street. He knew I didn't like surprises, especially in public. We continued eating then we left. That was my last Mother's Day with Kenny.

He was a proud daddy for the past three months; He lived every day talking about his son. Lil Kenny meant the world to him. He always talked about what they were going to do when he got older. One day he picked Lil Kenny up from Woodbridge where he lived with his mom. He said he was going to stop by his friend's house. I told him if you pick up the baby take him home, it was too cold to have him outside. Kenny was pretty good, about doing what I asked him to do. I called home an hour after he told me he was going home, I got no answer. I assumed he and Lil Kenny were asleep. I hung up the phone and returned to work. I decided to get off work a little early. I was excited about the baby being there. I couldn't wait to get home. My job was only five minutes from home.

I was coming into the driveway and saw a body quickly dash through the front door. I thought my eyes were playing tricks on me. Oh well maybe I was seeing things. I parked the car got out and went in the house. Just as I said Lil Kenny and Kenny were asleep. I went upstairs to change my clothes and to get comfortable. My daughter, Shundra, came in the room. I asked her how long Kenny and Lil Kenny had been asleep.

She said, "Ma, they're not asleep. Kenny just ran in the house. He jumped under the cover with Lil Kenny." She said, "Go downstairs and lift up the cover, they both are fully dressed. Lil Kenny still has on his snowsuit and Kenny had on his coat and timberline boots. He just has the cover pulled over them."

So my eyes were not playing games, it was somebody running in the house like I said. I went downstairs and pulled back the cover and they both were fully dress. Lil Kenny still had on his snowsuit and Kenny was fully dress. He laughed. I said, "Boy, I told you not to take the baby out; it is too cold."

He said, "I only took him around the corner." I was too happy to see Lil Kenny to be angry. I took the baby and undressed him. He was still asleep. Kenny sat next to me as I undressed Lil Kenny. He began telling me he couldn't wait to take Lil Kenny to get his first haircut and he was going to ride up front with him. He was so happy to have a son. A dream shattered. Lil Kenny and Shanae are both ten years old now.

It's been ten years and three months since Kenny's death and you know what; to this day my husband I continue to argue about the way I grieved over Kenny's death. I didn't know what to do. It breaks my heart to be reminded of how I grieved over Kenny. He reminded me how I went to the hospital a month after Kenny's death and left him and the children at home. I thought I was having a heart attack, what was I to do? He didn't understand the pain I was going through as a mother. He said I shouldn't have gone to the hospital. What was I supposed to have done? Die in front of my children? He said, "You should have come home." If I could have, I would have come home. I didn't know there was a home, I was grieving, and I was hurting. I had no control over how I was feeling. I felt he had a lot of animosity toward me and how I grieved over Kenny. I asked him, "Why are you so angry with me?" He said, "I wanted to have sex."

He felt our life was supposed to be the same a month after burying my son, my best friend. It couldn't be the same. I couldn't be the wife he once knew and wanted me to be. He felt months had gone by; our life should be back to normal. He didn't have the patience to understand I needed to get through this. He never said he understood and everything was going to be all right. He felt his needs were more important than my need to heal. My screams became silent in his presence. I couldn't allow him to hear me cry. He didn't support me mentally or emotional. I did it all by myself. Well not by myself but through the grace of the Almighty God.

He still tells me, to this day, I left my children. Even grieving, I supported each one of my children through high school, and Starla through two years of college. I was there physically and, most of the time, mentally. I did the best I could in the situation I was in. I was grieving, I was dying slowly. Can you imagine what it feels like to lose a child? His perception of death and mine were totally different. I couldn't understand my husband's perception of death, and he wasn't trying to understand me. I stopped trying to understand him because listening to him was disgusting.

To this day we still don't see eye to eye about death. He would always tell me, "You're holding on to Kenny." Yes, I am, that's the way I deal with his death, by holding on. If that's all I have left, why would he want to take that away? After seventeen years I still sometimes feel angry with God, my husband and sometimes even myself. I feel no one understands, and sometimes I wonder if anyone cares. I have made up my mind to try and live again, at least for now. Doing the right thing is the hardest thing in the world; the right thing is to try to live after the death of a child.

Chapter 13
Good Times

Kenny was a child who always wanted to be the center of all attention. He was a neat kid. He loved to scare you but he didn't want to be scared. I wanted to share with you some of our scariest moments.

I worked around the corner from the house, so I would come home and see his little car out front. That meant I was not home alone. I was afraid of being alone. I opened the door and yelled his name. He didn't answer, so I assumed he had ridden somewhere with one of his friend. I went into the kitchen to get something to drink, grabbed my bills and sat down. As soon as I sat down and kicked off my shoes, a hand touched me on my shoulder. I screamed and the bills went in the air, and so did my glass of whatever I was drinking. I ran toward the door before looking back to see who it was. He was bending over laughing so hard. I said, "Boy, you are going to get hurt doing stupid things like that." Oh he thought was so funny. He did a re-enactment of how I jumped up and ran. I was so mad. I said, "Boy, I am going back to work." He grabbed my hand still laughing and said, "I'm sorry," and I said, "No, I am going back to work." He followed me to the door still laughing. I looked back as he said, "I love you."

I said, "Uh." I went back to work and told my co-workers what he had done. They laughed and said your son is going to give you a heart attack.

Another episode of our good-times was when I was going downstairs to the laundry room across from his bedroom. I opened the door and yelled his name. He didn't answer so I called him again. I didn't get an answer, so I headed downstairs. I waited for a sound of feet. I didn't hear anything. I figured he must have left. I never bothered to look out front to see if his car was in the driveway. I got to the last step, peeped in his room and looked under his bed and in the closet. There was no sign of Kenny. Okay I am safe now. I walked into the laundry room, put down the laundry basket, opened the washer, put in the soap powder, closed the lid and turned around and there was Kenny standing behind me. I screamed. No one came to my rescue. They knew Kenny had done something. I told him I was not washing anymore clothes. He laughed. I loved every moment of the times we shared together. To know Kenny was to love Kenny. You couldn't help but to love him. He was that kind of child, that kind of friend, that kind of brother, that kind of son and that kind of dad. He would do anything to make you laugh.

Oh another good time I can recall. I came home again from work. This time I was more observant. I pulled in the driveway and saw his little red car. I said okay, that meant he was in the house. I opened the door and yelled his name. He didn't answer. I looked in the closet, behind the chair. I even went to the basement and yelled his name. I slammed the basement door, in case he came up the stairs, so I could hear the door opening. I figured this time he really was not home. I looked everywhere. I decided this time I would go to my bedroom and sit. There were no chairs, nothing you could hide behind.

I was walking and singing, looking down at each step I was taking. Literally I was counting the steps I was taking.

I got to the last step and saw a pair of big feet. I never looked up to see who they belonged to, I just starting screaming. He said, "Why are you yelling?"

I said, "What are you doing up here?"

He said, "I had to use the bathroom."

I said, "You heard me calling you."

He said, "I know" and ran down the steps. That was it I was not coming home anymore, I told him. When my co-workers asked what did he do this time, I just shook my head.

That was the last time I came home in a year. I stopped coming home, he started visiting me at work. He may be going somewhere with his friend, but he would always stop by and see me. It made my day whenever he came by. He was one of a kind. He was my friend.

The good times just keep coming. I have to share this one with you. One night my husband and I were asleep in bed. I woke my husband and told him, it sounded as though someone came in the house. We both lay there for a minute. We heard it again. I told him he may want to check it out. He got up. I jumped up behind him. I wanted to find out what it was. My husband's theory was to always leave the lights out when you hear something because nobody knows your house better than you. As he was creeping down the steps we heard it again. My husband continued creeping down the steps, taking them one by one. I was looking over the banister. If anything happened, I was going to run back into the bedroom and shut the door. He got to the last step and stopped and said, "Oh! Shit!" I knew he must have seen something.

I asked him what was wrong and he said, "Nothing." He later said as he stepped off the last step. He felt a body under his foot. Someone grabbed his ankle. He didn't want to scream and scare me. Good thing he didn't because I would have taken off running. It was Kenny lying at the bottom of the steps. He laid Kenny out.

He said, "Boy, you should have been somewhere sleeping." Kenny said he had just come in the house and knew I was probably listening, as I always did. Once he was in the house I would fall into a peaceful sleep. I knew he was dependable when locking the doors. He got that from my daddy. My daddy would lock a door and then stand there shaking it, almost breaking it off the hinges.

There were many good times. He has scared everybody. He asked me one day if he could have a dog. I said, "Boy, are you crazy? You cannot have a dog in here."

He laughed and said, "Why?"

I said, "Boy, you know I am afraid of dogs."

He said, "I'll keep him in the basement."

I said, "No!" and left it at that. I went back to the kitchen to continued cooking. After I finished cooking I walked into the living room and sat down. I saw something dark dart across the room. I ignored it, thinking I was seeing things. All of a sudden I saw the same shadow again.

I got up to go to the kitchen and there was a black shaggy dog. I ran out of the kitchen and jumped in the chair and stood on top of the table, screaming Kenny's name. They all took off running to find out what happened. I heard my younger son, Julius say, "Oh God where's the dog?" Kenny said, "Under the bed." I gathered he looked under the bed and the dog was gone. I looked up and there were Kenny, Julius, Shawn and a few of their friends. They all laughed because I was standing on the table. I told Kenny the dog came out of nowhere. He asked if the dog could stay the night. I said, "Yeah, but he has to go in the morning, and the basement door has to stay shut."

Every time I heard the basement door come open I ran. I called Kenny's name, he said, "Ma, the dog is under the bed."

I told him, "You told me that the last time."

He said, "I promise you he will not come back up here for the rest of the night." The dog didn't come back.

The next morning came, and I knew the dog had to leave. I wasn't sad at all. I was not going to be running around the house, at least not from a dog. He called my mom and asked if she wanted a dog. She was like me; she was afraid of dogs. She said she knew a friend of the family who might want it. He asked her to call and find out. Mama said she would call and let him know. He went back downstairs.

Within fifteen minutes the telephone rang and it was Mama. She said Ms. Brown would take him. He said to tell her I'd bring the dog today. After hearing that I stayed out of the way of the door possibly coming open. He showered and got dressed. He told the dog, "Baby, Mama don't love you." I looked at him as though he was crazy. He was leaving and said, "Tell Mama bye. I hurried up and shut the screen door. I didn't know where they were going. I just knew the dog was not in here. They went to Virginia Beach.

Let me tell you what he did to my mom. He walked into her room with a blanket as though he was carrying a baby. My mom asked him whose baby he was carrying. He said, "A friend of mine's." My mom, loving kids, asked him to let her hold the baby. He handed her the bundle. The dog was in the blanket. She saw the dog and said, "Boy, I'm going to get you." He was on the floor laughing. She called me. I laughed at her knowing what he had done to me. He took the dog to Mrs. Brown's house and that is where the dog is today.

His sister Shawn got him good one day. He was lying in the living room watching television. He said he heard something in the kitchen. He didn't get up and check because he knew the doors and windows were locked. He said he heard the same noise again. He decided to get up and check in the kitchen.

By time he got there all he saw was a head with all this hair. He didn't take time to find out who it was, all he knew was someone was coming through the kitchen window. He said he ran out the front door, almost through it. Out of breath, he banged on the neighbor's door across the street. By the time he got across the street, here comes Shawn. She had left her keys in the house and was coming in through the window. He was mad. They called me at work. I was glad somebody had finally scared him.

He got her back. She and her girlfriend had cut class. They decided to come to the house. They thought Kenny wasn't home. All of a sudden they heard something. They both ran into the closet. Knowing Kenny, he had already heard them walking around. He came upstairs, opened the closet door, and asked them what they were doing home. Shawn said she didn't know. He said, "Don't worry about it." He took them both back to school; she was embarrassed and angry with him for taking them back to school.

I remember when one time when my daughter Julia was asleep in the living room. Kenny put his other sisters and brothers up to putting hot sauce in her mouth. She always slept with her mouth open. She jumped up and started screaming. I was upstairs and didn't know what happened. I came downstairs and nowhere was Kenny to be found. He was always doing something. He was in his room with the cover over his head laughing. He said, "Man, I didn't do it. Shawn and Julius did it."

Chapter 14
The First Trial

Two months had gone by and I wasn't any better than I was when Kenny died. I was heading toward another devastation, the trial. I didn't know what to expect. Many people told me it would be devastating. The attorneys made you the perpetrator. I had never been to a trial. I didn't know what to expect. I had to talk with the district attorney who was handling the case. He told me to expect the worst. I couldn't expect the worst when the worst had already happened. Kenny was dead.

He informed me he would be calling me to go over the preliminary hearing to briefly discuss some of the details expected. I did and I didn't want to know. Knowing wouldn't bring Kenny back. Not knowing was unfair to Kenny. So to know was important.

He told me to call the office and set up an appointment with him. I called and spoke with his secretary. She was a very nice lady. She made me feel as though she knew me personally. She told me if I had questions feel free to call her, and if she wasn't available to leave a message and she would call me back. She held to her end of the bargain and so did I. The district attorney was fantastic. Whenever I called him he returned my call. So many people in that courthouse helped make my life a little easier. Kenny was dead. Everything was left up to me. I was finally told the names of the people who killed Kenny. I was eager to know.

Once I found their names, I start calling around, trying to find out if anyone knew them and why would they kill Kenny. No one seemed to know but the person who was with Kenny. He said he had been in a fight with the one who pulled the trigger. I wanted to know everything about him; where he lived, how old he was. I found it out in a short period of time. The one who was the accessory was seventeen years of age, and it was his birthday. I didn't care if they were ten and twelve. They killed Kenny, they destroyed a family, and they killed a dream. A dream that can no longer be fulfilled.

I wanted this trial to begin and end. I knew it was going to take awhile. I didn't have a while in my life. I needed closure, I needed peace, I needed to scream and I needed to put all of this behind me. The district attorney told me there would be two separate trials.

They try to degrade your loved one, because they can't defend themselves. There were two witnesses with Kenny when he was shot. I thanked God for them every day. I thanked God for their mothers who encouraged them to testify. Some parents don't want their children to testify, for fear they may get killed. Who wants to lose a child? I didn't, but I did. If my child were a witness, I would want him to testify. At least it would take a criminal off the streets and save another family from going through what I was going through...

Losing a child is one of life's most painful experiences. It leaves you so helpless. I couldn't imagine my child killed, never. I've seen it on television. I never dreamed I would be in the statistics of violent deaths. So many young children. I didn't think it could happen to me. It shows you that no matter who you are or where you live it can happen to you, because it happened to me.

I used to see it on the news. Mothers crying and children were dying. I couldn't imagine what they were going through; I couldn't imagine what they were feeling until it happened to me. After it happened to me, I screamed every time I heard a child was killed. I shared that mother's pain. I wanted to be there for her, I wanted to let her know, I knew her pain. I had to make a difference in someone's life, I had too. It was no longer about me. It was about helping someone else. I needed to.

I had to go through the trial; it was due to start in a week. I had already visited with the district attorney. He informed me where and what time the first trial was going to start. I reported to the first trial on Monday, March 19, 1990. I dreaded to wake up. I was going to, for the first time, see the person who not only killed Kenny, but killed a part of me.

The drive to the courthouse was at least twenty minutes. My husband, my children, my mom, my sisters and a few of his friends packed the courthouse on the first day of the trial. It was a cold day, not only the weather, but also facing a murderer. Someone who gave no value to life. I figured if he had any value to life he wouldn't have pulled the trigger to kill Kenny. He wouldn't have pulled the trigger to kill him. Not only did he destroy my life and his parents' lives. So many people were affected by this senseless murder.

We arrived at the courthouse. We had to walk through the metal detector. I had to empty my purse and I felt violated every time I walked into the courtroom. I felt I had no business there and neither did my family. The courtroom was cold, and so was the family on the opposite side of the courtroom. They acted as though I had killed their son. We were there for ten days and not one time did the mother of the accused child come to me with a comforting word. They never even made eye contact with me. Why? I couldn't understand.

They still had their child. What did I have but memories? At least they had been able to talk to their son, visit him in jail. What had I been able to do, but remember the last time I heard Kenny's voice. Being the person who I am, I would have gone over to her and apologized for what my son done. We as parents don't always know what our children will do. We have to pull together as parents and help one another. She wasn't responsible for what her son had done. I never once blamed her. I expected more from her as a parent.

We both were experiencing something very hard in our lives. She was going to be faced with having a child behind bars for the rest of her life, and I was going to be faced with not having my child for the rest of my life. Neither was going to be easy for either of us. I would change places with her. I would have rather visited my child in jail than in a cold cemetery. She was blessed and didn't realize it. I wondered how she went home and slept knowing a mother less than five feet from her was screaming because of the death of her child, when all she could have done was say the simple words, "I'm sorry" to help ease my pain a little.

Today was a long wasteful day. We had to wait for a jury to be picked, which could take at least another day or two or three. It took three days for a complete jury to be selected. We sat for three days in the same court room and never did his parents make eye contact. I began to wonder what kind of child he was. If a parent shows no remorse, how could the child have any? This speaks to why this child could go out and kill so easily. If the parents don't care, how could the child care? We have to set examples for our children. No matter what they do we have to be parents. That was one thing I was told in the preliminary you would feel as though you were the one who did something wrong. I felt that way for weeks and months. I had no reason to.

I prayed this would be quick. I needed closure to this nightmare. Closure is a hard word to use. There is no closure after the death of a child, in the courtroom there were so many police officers passing me. I wondered who they were and what purpose did they have in this trial. I screamed silently. I didn't know if they were affiliated with this trial or not. It didn't matter. One officer was carrying a gun in a brown paper bag. I wondered if it was the gun used to kill Kenny. I wanted to jump up and run out of the courtroom. Another officer had a brown bag which I later found out had Kenny's clothes in it. Why was he carrying this bag? After learning that, I stopped being suspicious of the officers passing by. I no longer wanted to know. I didn't know that many people were involved in the case.

There were officers who secured the crime scene, there were officers who were the first to arrive on the scene, and there were officers who shined the helicopter light on the scene. Everybody had a part but me. The only part I had in this was to bury my child and a part of me.

While sitting there waiting on the jury to be picked, a very special lady confronted me. She headed a very special group for the entire Prince George's County. The name of the cooperation is Parents of

Murdered Children. In spite of her own daughter being murdered brutally, she sat in the courtroom with me holding my hand. I needed someone who knew the way I was feeling. I needed to know I wasn't the only one who lost a child. Even though you see children dying every day, you still feel alone, you feel no one knows the pain you are in. She made a big difference in my life. She told me if she didn't make it every day someone from her staff would be there with me. Every one of her staff members had lost a child to a violent murder. It truly helps to know someone understands your cry. They were there every day. They sat next to me holding my hand as I cried silently.

The trial was to begin on Thursday, the jury having been selected. Tomorrow meant putting a face to the name of the person who killed Kenny. I had heard the names for weeks and months. I left the courthouse with a little relief. No more in a courtroom with policeman whispering.

Thursday morning came. The metal detectors no longer intimidated me. I was finally going to see the person who was responsible for killing Kenny. We were told to return to the courtroom at 9:00 a.m., of course we were there by 8:30 a.m... The judge was late as he had been for the last three times we were in court. I was tired of the phrase, *All Rise*. I did rise but my body stayed down. I felt too heavy to rise, not from weight but from the grief that had been imposed on me. I was struggling day by day.

I was sitting on the front row of seats in the courtroom, shaking and feeling as though every muscle in my body was doing its own thing. At one point I was crying and didn't even know it. I played with my hands like a child. That was what I felt like. I wanted to be as close to the front as I could. I didn't want to miss anything that was said. I wanted to hear why they killed Kenny. Not only that, I wanted to get a good look at the person who was responsible for the disaster in my life.

The door opened and so did my heart. I saw him. He came in dressed as though he had done no wrong to anyone. He was very arrogant. He had no care in the world. He looked at me as though, yeah, I did it. I screamed silently. I wanted to get up and scream. I couldn't because if I did they would put me out of the courtroom. I needed to be there, not for me but for Kenny. I promised Kenny in the hospital I would see to it that the person who did this would pay. I had to keep my promise, so I screamed silently. He was a medium built, attractive young man; such a waste of his life. I couldn't hate him. I was angry. Angry that he not only wasted Kenny's life but his life too.

I remembered those police officers I had seen earlier; they were witnesses on the case.

They called the first officer to the stand. He was the first to arrive on the scene. He was a tall, brown skinned young man, well built. He looked like he had been working out for days. He secured the area so none of the evidence would be disturbed. I didn't know him but I thanked God somebody was there with Kenny. Kenny meant nothing to this officer, only to me. He was doing his job, but I thanked God for him. He said when he arrived on the scene there was a Black man lying on the ground with what seemed to be multiple gunshot wounds.

I screamed silently, yet a tear trickled down my face at the thought of Kenny laying on a cold ground bleeding to death. This was one time I was hoping he was in shock. In shock, you felt no pain. I hoped he was. The officer said it was kind of dark so he had to call for emergency lighting equipment to take pictures of the area and Kenny. The thought of a camera flashing in your face while you're lying in a pool of your own blood isn't what most of us would want. I know he didn't want it but he had no choice. At somebody else's choice, there my child lay; not even a mother could help. After listening to that first testimony, as soon as he stepped down, I jumped up and ran out the courtroom, crying, trying hard to make it to the bathroom. Before I got there, the tears were no longer silent. I opened the door and slid to the floor crying. What I had just heard was enough.

I had to be strong in spite of what I just heard. I promised Kenny I would be there through the end. I got up off the floor, washed my face, and went back into the courtroom. I had too far to go to break down now.

The next witness who took the stand was the paramedic who arrived to administer emergency treatment to Kenny. She said when she arrived at the scene she found a young Black man with multiple gunshot wounds. I asked myself if she had to be so graphic. I guess to get a point across to the jurors she had to. She said, "One wound was above the left side of the upper back, and one wound was on the left thigh." I screamed again saying to myself, *Why me?* She said he was "grave dead" when she arrived.

I screamed again silently. I remembered the doctor at the emergency room telling me when I got there Kenny was okay. I began to wonder how he could have been okay after listening to this paramedic. She said when she found him he was "grave dead." Who was lying, the doctor or the paramedic? I cried, I couldn't understand. Then I had to calm down and remember. Maybe he was near death and she stabilized him. That was the best I could come up with.

She began to say there was a large hole in the front of his chest. I screamed again and again silently. I felt I was dying right before the eyes of the jurors and my family. I had so many silent tears backed up in my head I felt I would cry forever. I couldn't take hearing anymore yet I couldn't leave.

The suspect never showed any remorse whatsoever. He had a smirk on his face. I wondered where his heart was or did he even have one. I looked over at his family as his sister put her head down in disbelief.

Continuing the testimony from the look of the wounds Kenny had sustained, she suggested to the paramedic who was assisting her to call for a helicopter for Kenny to be transported to the hospital. He wouldn't have made it if he had gone by ambulance. The closest ambulance was less that a block from the scene. The ambulance arrived to take Kenny to the helicopter; the landing field was up the street from where he was shot.

One of Kenny's closest friends, Tina, was there the entire time. She said when the ambulance doors opened they were still working on Kenny until the helicopter arrived. Once they arrived the med star unit took over. I painfully remembered I was at the corner of my house talking to a police officer while they were taking care of him. He telephoned the scene and asked if I could come up there. They said no he was in route to the hospital. I wanted to know where they were taking him. The officer called back and said he was being flown to the hospital.

We jumped in the car and headed to the hospital. I asked the officer who was a neighborhood friend how bad Kenny was. He said it didn't look good, and I screamed right before his eyes, but silently. He patted me on my shoulder. I left for the hospital.

Hearing this in the courtroom only brought back memories. I remembered that incident very well. After the paramedic got off the witness stand, it was close to lunchtime. I figured the judge was going to break. He did. He said this would be our last witness for the morning. Court would adjourn until 1 p.m. I knew he must have meant 1:30 because he hadn't been on time since the trial began two days ago. I didn't care. I wanted to get out of the courtroom anyway. It was too much drama for me. Too much heartache, too much of everything. I didn't know if I was going to make it through this trial, much less the second one.

We left the courtroom with the intention of having lunch. Instead we spent most of our time consoling each other. It was hard for all of us. Everyone was concerned about me. I was ready to give up, I was ready to die. I cried this time openly to my mom. I told her I couldn't take it. She said, "You know Kenny wouldn't want you to give up."

I though for a moment, he gave up, why can't I? He didn't give up by choice. I dried my teary eyes enough to go on to the cafeteria. Everybody was hungry, including me but I couldn't eat. I wanted to hurry back to the court and let the day be over. I wanted to sleep; I wanted to forget about the trial and all I had been through. I had no peace and I was tired.

They ordered a sandwich and a soda, something that was quick for everyone. We only had thirty minutes left. I used those thirty minutes to cry. I was sorry, but I could no longer be strong for my family. We had about five minutes left to make it back to the court but it wouldn't have mattered; I knew the judge was going to be late.

We hurried to the courtroom, only to face an empty room. No jurors, no judge, no bailiff, and last but not least, not the person who killed Kenny. We sat quietly for five minutes before the all-to-familiar voice said, "All Rise." The door opened and so did my heart. In came the young man who shattered my life, still in handcuffs and shackles. I did what I had done most of the day; I stared at him and wondered why? Why did he shoot Kenny in the back as he ran for his life, why? I wondered how could you shoot a man with his back turned. All the things that raced through my mind wouldn't bring Kenny back, so I had to put those thoughts to rest. I sat quietly and patiently for the next witness.

The next witness was the doctor, who spent nine hours in the operating room trying to save Kenny, losing him twice and reviving him, only for him to die anyway. I knew he did all he could have done. It was not his fault. He didn't shoot Kenny. He walked up to the stand raised his right hand and swore under oath to tell the whole truth and nothing but the truth. He walked around to the chair that faced the assailant and me. I remembered talking to him in the emergency room. He was just as hurt as I was.

He began his testimony with a chart and a stick. He began to demonstrate where the bullets had entered Kenny's body and the damage they had done. My body was numb now. He said, "As Kenny was running, one bullet struck him in the back, piercing his lung." He bent over in the position he was running. He then pointed to the wound in the back of the leg that struck the scrotum, and the other one tore a part of his colon. He said he operated on Kenny for nine hours. He had to stop twice because he started to bleed severely in the lung that was damaged, which eventually caused him to remove the total right lung. He couldn't stop the bleeding.

I sat and sat as long as I could. I felt my heart was being ripped out of my body right before the judge, the jurors, my family, and God. I jumped up and ran out of the courtroom. I didn't cry. I wanted to but I couldn't because I didn't want his family to think I was trying to get sympathy from the jury. I walked to the nearest ladies room and sat on the floor and cried and cried. I could no longer take this anymore. I wanted to die. I knew God understood.

This lady who was in the ladies room washing her hands came over to help me. I couldn't get up my, body was too heavy.

I was dressed in a beautiful deep purple suit with a white shirt, sitting on the floor. I looked up and there was my mom. She took my hand and tried to help me. I buried my head in her chest and cried, "Oh, Mama, no! Please, I can't do it. I want to die." She began to recite the 23rd Psalm. Not that I didn't appreciate what she was doing, it just wasn't working for me. I knew I had to get back into the courtroom. She turned on the water and washed my face. Feeling as helpless as ever, I couldn't hide the sad look over my face. I couldn't hide the puffy red eyes. I didn't care any more who saw me. Why did I have to hide my pain anymore? He didn't hide his when he killed Kenny. My child was the one murdered. I had every reason to scream.

I went back to my seat and continued listening to the trial. The doctor was no longer using the pointer; he was sitting in his seat. I missed a part of it. I didn't need to know what I missed. I knew one thing I missed Kenny. After about five more minutes of testimony, the day was over. I was glad. I needed to go home. I needed to lie down; I felt I needed to die. I didn't know who was going to testify tomorrow or what they were going to say. I knew I needed to leave now. I felt I couldn't breathe. I began to hyperventilate, I needed air.

I left the courtroom before the bailiff could say, "All Rise." I was gone. I was standing out front. We only had one more day and it would be the weekend. That meant no courtroom, no metal detectors, no police officer, and no judge. For the first time I was looking forward to the weekend, even though I had no plans. My body needed the rest and my mind had already worked overtime. Before looking forward to the weekend, I had to get past Friday, the last day of the trial at least until Monday. I had two days to regroup and prepare for not a two-day trial but a week long trial. Remember, this trial started Thursday, ending on Friday. The next trial was to start Monday and end on Friday. An entire week.

I dreaded the days to come; I dreaded the week of sitting in front of the child who killed Kenny. I no longer had to wonder what he looked like. I wanted to know then, now I didn't. We got on the bus that took us to our cars. You see, going to court there is no place to park. You have to park and ride. I didn't want to park and ride the bus, but I had no choice. It took us only three minutes.

After arriving at the parking lot I stepped off the bus with the weight of the world on my shoulders. My feet seemed to be the heaviest of all. We all got in the car heading home. In my mind I was heading in a different direction. I was on my way to the cemetery. It was a cold, windy evening. I should have been going home to a nice warm house; instead I went to a cold cemetery. Kenny had only been gone for three months to this day. Kenny was shot on a Friday and died on a Friday, and I was on my way to the cemetery on a Friday.

I went home with my family and pretended I needed to go to the store. They believed it. No one ever knew what was on my mind but me. I hid so much pain and grief from my family. I was too hurt; I was too ashamed to let them know. I don't know why I felt ashamed. I did nothing wrong. The person who killed him should be feeling what I was feeling. Instead he had a half smile on his face. On the way home from the court I saw his face. I hated that look he had. He knew I hated it and I thought that was why he did it. He made it so obvious his attorney told him to keep his head straight and sit up.

I drove on to the cemetery, crying loudly, telling Kenny I loved him. I was crying so uncontrollably I thought I was going to crash. I could not see for the tears. I no longer cared about me, only God did. He was the only one. I turned into the cemetery; it was getting a little dusty and very windy. I stopped the car and took in a deep breath. I laid my head back and cried, "Oh, Kenny, I miss you so much, baby." Tears rolled down my face. I opened the door and got out. I headed toward his grave. I sat down on the stone next to Kenny. I buried my head in my lap and continued to cry. I removed my hand only to be looking down at a pair of men's shoes. I was not afraid. I didn't care.

Whoever this person was I was about to see I never heard him come up. I never heard footsteps; I never heard a car door shut.

I looked up and saw a medium build, attractive young Black man. He said, "Hello."

I said, "Hi."

He said, "Who are you visiting?"

I couldn't talk for the tears. I said softly, "My son."

He asked me what happened, and I told him Kenny was murdered. He wanted to know how old he was and I told him nineteen years old. He said, "Oh, he was rather young."

I put my head down and said, "Yeah, I know." He asked how long had he been dead. I said, "Oh, about three months now." He looked startled.

I asked him was there a problem and he said, "Yeah." He said, "Looking at his gravesite it seems maybe a week ago." I asked him why he would say that. He said, "The dirt is too new."

I said, "Maybe he wanted it like that so I could always find him."

He said, "No, that's not what it is." I asked him then what. He said, "It means Kenny is not at rest. You are holding on."

I said, "Yes, I am."

He said, "You've got to let go so he can rest." He didn't know the relationship Kenny and I had.

We continued to talk, and he began to share with me how his parents died. My heart went out to him. I couldn't relate to his pain since both of my parents were still living. I listened. But letting go of Kenny was the last thing I wanted to hear. I was so out of it that when he asked me to sit in his car I did. If I had been in the right state of mind, I would have never got in anyone's car. He had something to show me. Danger never entered my mind and I guess I didn't care.

I walked over to his car, opened the passenger's door, got in, and closed the door. He could have been a murderer. I continued talking to him, never realizing I knew nothing about this man. He could have killed me and no one would have known. I guess I talked to anyone who would listen to me. Not that I didn't think I could talk to my family, but they didn't understand my pain. I turned to a stranger.

I later found out who this man was. He worked in the office at the cemetery and he counseled people after the death of a loved one. You see how good God is? I was never alone. I felt God had sent an angel to watch over me. He knew the pain I was in. He said he would never leave me. I got out of his car and he walked me to my car. He gave me a card and told me whenever I needed to talk to call him. He gave me a hug and opened my car door and I got in and drove off. I was never afraid of this man. I don't know why.

I left the cemetery. I called home to let my family know I was okay. Of course they wanted to know where I was, where had I been. I told them the truth. My sister Jack asked why I went alone. I told her, "I didn't go alone." She asked what did I mean by that, and I told her while I was there sitting on the tomb next to Kenny, a man appeared out of nowhere. She yelled and asked if I was crazy. I told her, "No, who cared." I began to cry again. I didn't care. I wanted to die. I felt if this total stranger could see me grieving, so should my family.

I could no longer see the road, the tears were pouring. I pulled in the parking lot of a grocery store and laid my head back on the seat and cried. I cried for ten minutes. I didn't think I was going to make it. The pain was too much to bear. I missed Kenny so much. I felt I couldn't go on. I was tired of crying. I sat up and wiped my face, but the tears started again. I needed to go home but I couldn't, not like this. I couldn't pray, not just yet. I know what I needed to do; I needed to pray. I couldn't. How could I? How could I ask God for anything right now. I was angry with God for letting Kenny die. I refused to ask, I was hoping my anger would cause God to let me die.

It didn't. I had begun to give up on waiting for God to take me. I wanted to be with Kenny whatever it took to be there. I was ready, other than suicide. My mom said if I did that I would never see him. I managed to pull myself together enough to take a five-minute drive to my house.

I pulled into the driveway and before I could turn off the car the front door came opened. It was my daughters Pooh and Starla. They worried more about me than I did. I went into the house only to be questioned where I had been. My big mouth sister Jack called and told my husband where I was. He said, "You think nobody cares about you." I hunched my shoulder, it didn't matter if anyone cared about me, the pain was too deep, and it hurt too bad. I had no room in my life to worry about who cared about me.

I went upstairs to my room. I was very distant from my family, but not intentionally. I looked back over the years and I hurt even worse knowing I hurt them. I didn't mean to. I was a disaster I was a walking time bomb, waiting to explode anytime. I sat on the bed thinking about the trial coming up on Monday. I couldn't rest. I was afraid. I didn't know who was going to testify next.

I felt I was the victim; why me? I had gone through enough. I began to question myself, I began to blame myself, I began to hate myself. I lay back in the bed with my hands under my head staring in the ceiling asking, God, Why? Again no answer. I was tired of getting no answer.

What had I done to deserve this? What had Kenny done in his short life to die like this?

I hated my life and everything around it. I needed to sleep.

I couldn't sleep without the help of Zanax, an anti depressant. I liked the way it made me feel. It helped me sleep and forget about the pain and relax and the loneliness that rested upon my heart. It put me in a deep sleep. A sleep sometimes I didn't want to come out of. When I slept I saw Kenny and that was what I wanted. I slept for hours. I tried to stay asleep. If someone woke me up, I would become very angry, because waking up to reality was the hardest thing to accept. I would take them faithfully to sleep. I remember one night I misplaced them. I cried, afraid I would have to stay awake. I knew Monday was coming and I had to go back to the place I hated the most, the court.

I tried to sleep all day Sunday dreading Monday. I walked the floor, I couldn't sleep. I wanted to scream. I was wondering how did the person that killed Kenny sleep. I couldn't sleep and I hadn't killed anyone. I wonder now that he had seen my face did it bother him. He has a mother, would he want her to hurt like this. What was he thinking about over the weekend knowing he could spend the rest of his life in jail or did he care?

I was finally able to sleep through the night. I had set the clock for 6:00 a.m. It seemed six o'clock came sooner than I wanted. The clock went off and I turned over and shut it off, and lay in the bed staring at the ceiling, wondering how I was going to make it through this trial. I was nervous and scared. I couldn't move, and I couldn't pray. I thanked God for being an understanding and caring God. I got up and went into the bathroom and showered. I turned on the water and began to cry. I didn't want to go back to the court. I didn't want to see the person who killed Kenny. I didn't want to see the policeman, I didn't want to see the judge, and I didn't want to see the jurors. I didn't want to see anyone. I wanted this day to end. I wanted to scream. I had no choice. I promised Kenny I would see to it this person would be punished. If I died doing anything it would be doing what I promised him.

We dressed and left to do the usual; first get coffee. Then we headed to the courthouse, which was twenty-five minutes away at the most. This was one day I was hoping would never start. I remembered what I heard in court on Thursday and Friday. I wasn't in a hurry to hear that again. I felt I was the victim. Listening to the paramedic and the doctor's testimony drained every ounce of energy I had in my body. I wondered who was going to testify today and what I was going to hear. I asked myself if it could be any worst than what I had already heard. The worst of it was when the paramedic said Kenny was grave dead when she got there. The testimony was even more devastating when the doctor said Kenny died twice on the table. I asked God, "How much more can I take?"

It was 8:50 a.m. And we were on the bus en route to the court. The thought of entering the courtroom and looking at this boy who killed Kenny caused me to scream silently. The bus stopped so did my heart. My sister hunched me and told me to get up. I didn't want to. I felt like a child going to school for the first time, frightened. I stepped off the bus and tried to mentally prepare myself for the today. I couldn't no matter how hard I tried.

We entered through the metal detector and walked to the information desk to find out if we were in the same courtroom.

According to the district attorney sometimes they switched courtrooms. We found it and nothing was different. The judge was still late. The bailiff was standing in the same spot he was in on Friday. I wondered if they went home. I stared at the surrounding in this courtroom it was smaller. That meant the defendant would be closer to me.

I wanted to jump over the rail in the last two days and choke him. No matter what I felt I wanted to do to him it would never be compared to what he did to Kenny. If I did anything I wouldn't be able to stay in the courtroom. I wouldn't be able to keep my promise to Kenny.

While sitting there I was watching everybody that went by. I glanced over at the defendant's family; they seemed to be at peace. His parents and two sisters were there. Being a mother, I expected more from her. She never made eye contact with me. We both were hurting but in a different way.

The door came open; my thoughts about what she should have done disappeared. It was no longer about her. In came the jurors one by one. They looked fresh and ready. Why would they look and feel different? Kenny meant nothing to them and neither did the defendant. The bailiff said, "All rise." I stood up my body stayed down. In came the judge. He opened the case file and read off the defendant's name. Within seconds a door came open and in came the defendant.

He looked no more concerned than he did on Thursday and Friday. While locked up over the weekend, seeing his family, did it give him any remorse for what he did? I don't think anything mattered to him. He had this arrogant attitude about himself. He acted as though what he did no was big deal.

Maybe he had no value to life. If it was me I would have been looking sad, pleading for the jurors to see it was an accident, I was sorry. This child didn't realize his attitude played a huge part on his life.

Court was ready to begin. The next witness, a police office who secured the area, and took pictures at the scene was called. He said it was dark and he called for special equipment to light the area. He took pictures of Kenny lying on the ground mortally wounded and the area in which he lay. His testimony was short and devastating to me and my family and anyone who has a child. If it wasn't for this arrogant idiot there would have been no trial. The policeman was on the stand for five minutes. I was glad.

The prosecutor wasted no time calling the next witness; the coroner. He came through the gate stood before the bailiff, raised his right hand and swore to tell the truth and nothing but the truth. What did he have to swear to; Kenny was already dead when he took over. His testimony was short but heart breaking for me being Kenny's mother. He testified as to which wound was deadly. He said, "The bullet that penetrated the lung caused the fatal wound." He said, "Kenny had eaten a half hour before he was shot which caused food to spill into the stomach area and cause severe damage to his organs." He went so far as to say Kenny had a drink of grape soda.

He was supposed to go to dinner later that night. He had called me at work and told me he was taking a girl name Robin out to dinner. I gathered he grabbed something before going to dinner. I wondered if he had not eaten would it have made a difference. Well it's too late for me to worry about the "what ifs," Kenny was dead. It was so hard to say Kenny was dead.

It was eleven thirty and I knew we only had time for one more witness. Who was it going to be? It was the detective I had been talking to since the capture of the two defendants. I thanked God for him. He didn't have too much to say, no more than he was the detective assigned to the case. The before picture that he asked me to take would have been showed to the jurors if Kenny had lived. The before pictures will have shown Kenny hooked up on a respirator, tubes in his throat, and the catheter that was hooked beneath him. It was a sad site for a mother to see her child like this. None of us expected Kenny to die, at least not me

The next witness to take the stand was the key witness to the murder. He had been threatened before testifying. He was told if he testified he would be sorry. It didn't bother him. I was afraid at one point he was going to back out. He walked into the courtroom more confident than any of the witnesses. He raised his right hand and swore to tell the truth and nothing but the truth. He took the witness stand, and the defendant stared at him. He ignored his stares and testified very well.

He said the two defendants were walking behind them, and they stopped to let them by. Kenny asked if he had seen these guys before and the witness said yeah. He had an altercation with the shorter one, who was the accessory in the case. Kenny felt confident that it was okay to continue his walk to the store. As they got to the end of the path there stood the same two guys again. One was pretending to tie his shoes, while the other one was leaning against a porch.

Just as Kenny and his friends approached the narrow path, the defendant stood up with a gun pointing at Kenny. He asked for Kenny's coat and watch. Kenny took off the coat and watch, and handed them to him.

He said, "Kenny then looked at me and we decided to take a chance and run. We did but in different directions. The defendant began shooting at Kenny. I didn't know if Kenny had been shot but I ran to a neighbor's house and called my mother, who told me to call 911. I ran back to where we were. That's when I realized Kenny had been shot. I stayed there with him until the ambulance got there."

The district attorney asked do you see the person who shot Kenny in the court room. The witness pointed to the defendant. He stared at me as he walked down off the stand.

I was very proud if him. If it wasn't for him being with Kenny, there could have been another mother going through what I'm going through. The defendant's attorney drilled this child bad, but he never backed down. I thought why should this child be drilled? He didn't pull the trigger that killed Kenny. The person who should have been drilled was sitting at the defendant's table with an attitude of so what. Put him on the stand and release this innocent child. Instead they continued questioning the witness. He showed a little nervousness and began to play with his hands. That was okay. He continued to stand firm on who killed Kenny. I knew his mom was afraid someone would retaliate on her son and so was I. God only knows I didn't want her or any other mother to go through what I was going through.

It was getting late in the evening and I knew he would be the last witness for the day, and he was. After his testimony the judge told him to return tomorrow, and to not discuss his testimony with anyone. He stepped down. I wanted to run over and hug him. His testimony convinced me, so I knew he convinced the jurors that this person in the front of the courtroom did indeed kill Kenny.

I'm sorry, so sorry, to say that Ramon is dead. He too was killed so senselessly. He was killed as violently as Kenny. I hurt all over again. He was like a son to me just like Kenny was like a son to his mom.

There were two people with Kenny when he was shot. The other person would testify tomorrow. He was very nervous. I hoped he held up. He too was threatened. I believe he was afraid for his life, more than Ramon.

The day ended with Ramon's testimony. We left the courtroom as tired as ever. I was mentally drained and doing what I have been doing for the past months, screaming silently. This was the first time I wanted to go home and rest. I felt I had no home. I felt helpless. It seemed as though the court was my home. I spent more time in the courtroom than I did at home.

The ride home as okay. We all felt that this person who was responsible for Kenny's death would not walk free, I had promised Kenny that I would make sure whoever did this to him would pay. I felt with the testimony I had heard I was confident he wasn't going to see the street anymore or hurt anyone else's child. No other mother will have to scream silently as I have.

I went home to prepare myself for tomorrow by taking a Zanax, a pill that kept me alive. I needed to rest. I cried silently. I was beginning to feel timid from the ongoing cross examinations. Why? I asked. These kids were innocent. They tried so hard to confuse the witnesses. The defendant sat through it all and never one time was he crossed examined. If it wasn't for him this trial wouldn't be going on, yet he's sitting back like he did nothing at all. I fell asleep and didn't wake up until the next morning. I was in such a deep sleep I thought this was all just a bad dream.

I had a dream about Kenny and it seemed real. When I woke up I was angry because I realized it was only a dream. Kenny was still dead. I sat on the side of the bed and screamed silently. I know I saw him. I hated to wake up out of the dreams that involved Kenny. I got really sad when reality sat in. I could have slept for hours, days, months, and even years, rather than live my life without Kenny. The pain it hurt so badly. I didn't feel any one needed me anymore. I felt I was good for nothing. I failed Kenny. I let him die. I prayed and prayed and he still died.

The sun had come up and that meant another day at the court, another day looking at the defendant, an arrogant person who made me want to scream, and another day of that stupid metal detector. I couldn't worry about that, I had to get dressed and go to do a chore that I hated so much.

A chore I promised my dying child. A promise I must keep. I promised Kenny I would stand in his absence and I knew God was going to see me through.

We took the usual route, going to the 7-Eleven and getting coffee. I wondered if it was the coffee that kept me going. I had become dependent on stopping for coffee every day. One day we missed getting coffee and I felt nervous. It could have just been me. Today we only had time to go through the metal detector and find the courtroom. Again they had changed the courtroom. I didn't really want to go anyway, but there was no other choice for me. I had to go regardless. We walked down this long hallway, only to find out we had to move again. I was tired, tired of everything now. Nothing mattered anymore. I was crying silently. So silently that not my mom, my husband, my children or the defendant knew. Only God and I heard my silent screams. He heard my cries. He comforted my heart when no one knew I was hurting. I thanked God every day for watching over me.

I didn't know how long this trial was going to be, or if I would live to the end of it. The days got harder. We were winding down with witnesses. I was glad.

The next witness was a very good friend of Kenny's. I looked at him and my heart went out to him, because he was nervous, while he was standing there with his hand up swearing under oath. I prayed, hoping he would hold up at least until after the trial. He never looked at the defendant. He too played with his hands as he testified. I can only imagine how he was feeling, testifying in front of a lot of people. Some of the questions I figured he should be able to answer, but he stumbled. I cried silently, hoping and praying he didn't quit now. I needed this testimony and so did Kenny. I thought for a moment, Oh God please don't let this boy walk free who killed Kenny. I prayed harder than I ever had.

When they asked him if the person who shot Kenny was in the courtroom, he never made eye contact. He was scared for his life. If I could have protected him I would. After his testimony he stepped down almost tripping from nervousness. I looked at him and nodded, letting him know he did well.

It was time for lunch again. I wish there were no lunch breaks. Lunch breaks made me sad. I wanted this trial to end. I knew people had to eat. Everyone didn't love Kenny like I did. Kenny was my child and I felt it wasn't a concern to anyone other than me. I had a very selfish love of my child. Lunch may have been important to them just as Kenny was to me.

I sat and stared and wondered why we couldn't just get this over. I sat and cried, staring at the seat occupied by the defendant. I was in a daze for a minute before I realized it, everyone was waiting on me.

I got up. We walked over to the cafeteria and as usual had lunch. I didn't want to eat; my mom said to me, "You have to eat. That is the only way you are going to be strong for Kenny and this trial." I sat and watched everyone else order all kinds of food. I couldn't eat. I wanted to go back to the court so I could go home. The time seemed to be moving.

It was time to return to the courtroom. I was the first one to enter. I wanted to get this over so I could go on with my life, which had been on hold since December 29, 1989, and it was now March. I needed to put closure to this trial. I felt my life was slowly, slipping away. We sat for ten minutes before the judge came in. I didn't need any extra minutes. I wanted to start now.

I heard the door open and it was the judge entering. The door opened again, and it was the defendant, looking just as unconcerned as he was before he left. I thought at least he ate. Kenny could never eat again. I began feeling sorry for myself. I had every right to. I brought Kenny into this world, why should he make the choice of taking him out.

The witness was called, someone I never seen or heard of. He walked over to the witness stand and took a seat. I whispered to my husband, "Who is that?" He didn't know either. I figured we would have to wait to find out what he knew. I remembered the District Attorney telling me there were a few other witnesses who saw what happened.

The district attorney asked him where he was on December 29 at approximately 7:30. He stated he was sitting in his car. He asked what he was doing. He said he was talking on the telephone to a co-worker. He asked what unusual thing happened. He said he heard gunshots, but he kept on talking. He said he looked up and Kenny was standing there holding his chest. He said Kenny dove through his window, landing in his lap. He said he opened the car door and helped him, by placing him on the ground. The attorney asked him if he knew Kenny and he said, "Yeah." That was the end of his testimony. He never saw who shot Kenny.

He stepped down and I cried, no longer silently. I let the tears stream down my face. I no longer cared who heard my cries. At one point I looked at the jurors and one lady was looking at me, as though she knew the pain I must have been in. I felt she knew something. She just stared sadly.

He was the last witness for this trial. I wanted to find this witness. I needed to thank him. He helped me to know Kenny was not alone. I left the courtroom and hurried out the door. I caught up with him and hugged him and thanked him. To know he was there to help Kenny, he held him last. I cried as I hugged him.

I went home and cried myself to sleep. At the thought of Kenny, diving through a window. He must have been in shock. I was hoping and praying and wondering to this day, did Kenny suffer? I wanted to know and I didn't want to. It will always be in my mind, whether I want it to be or not.

My family caught up with me and we got up on the bus to go home. A place I didn't want to go. On the way home, the car was completely quiet. I think everybody was focused on what we had heard at the end of the trial. It was devastating, heartbreaking, and sad to know that my child, their nephew, her grandson, their brother, their cousin, and their father had to dive through a car window after being shot. I cried for hours after leaving the court today.

After arriving home from the end of a sad day, I could only sit on the closest chair my body would allow me to. I felt like dropping to the floor and screaming as loud as I could. I couldn't it would hurt so many people around me. The thought of my children only allowed me to scream silently.

Everyone seemed to be ready to fall back into their usual routine. I felt cheated. I could only sit in a corner and cry silently. It wasn't what I chose to do; it was all I could do. I knew nothing else to do. Knowing this was just the first trial. The thought of having to repeat this over again brought much pain to my heart. I said over and over to myself, "I can't do it again." My faith was very faint. I knew God would be the only one who would be able to carry me through this. How? I was too angry with God to ask for help. I felt God let Kenny die. I couldn't quite understand the power of God. I had to learn to trust in God again, but not right now.

I headed toward the steps. I looked up. There were fifteen steps facing me, and I wondered, "Oh God! How am I going to make it up there?" My body felt too heavy to walk. I needed to go to my bedroom and get away from everyone just for a minute. I needed to cry. I managed to make the first step and God helped me the rest of the way. I have a strong belief in God. I was left with little choice but to believe. He understood even though I was angry with him, he never left me.

Who else could carry me through what I have been through? Who else could keep me from losing mind but God? The road I've traveled thus far has been so rough. I wondered if there would ever be a good time again.

The trial was to resume on Monday. I felt I couldn't begin to live until all of this was behind me. Every day for the past days, weeks and months I had nothing but memories, memories of Kenny. Sad moments crying and wanting to die. How I was going to make it only God knew. Yet I was too angry to ask God.

I got up Monday morning with the weight of the world on my shoulder. I dreaded to go back to the cold court room to face the person who destroyed my life. I had to go back.

It was the end of the trial that had been going on for a week. I was tired.

We left home around 7:30 a.m. as though I was on my way to work. I think many a days as much as I wanted not to be at work, I would have chosen to be there than where I was heading. I wouldn't or couldn't imagine anyone wanting to go where I was. I didn't want to be there. The morning ritual came, the same thing. Entering the courtroom. Walking to the front of the courtroom. I couldn't sit in the back. I needed to hear everything. I needed to know why this monster killed Kenny. I never found out even though I was sitting in the front of the courtroom. All I knew was Kenny was dead. I thanked God we knew who did it and I wanted him to pay. So many people are murdered and the family doesn't even get to have a trial, no witnesses.

I seemed to be complaining but I thanked God every day for the witnesses in this case. I don't know what I would have done if there was no witness. No matter what happened it wouldn't bring Kenny back. There was no victory to come out of this trial; the only good to come out of this trial was that this person would never be able to hurt another family as he did mine.

The trial was winding down, yet I had another trial to face. Another week in the court, looking at the doctors, paramedics, and policemen. I asked God, "How am I going to do this?" I screamed silently. I felt like a child who was being made to do something she didn't want to do. I had barely made it through the first trial. It was over today. I finally would be able to go home and try to keep my head up. I felt no one really understood my pain, so I continued to hide it. I had hidden this pain so deep inside me I almost killed myself. I was grieving silently. I may have thought it was silently, my body was telling me different. I felt faint, nervous and scared. You name it I felt it.

This trial ended today. Yet I had no idea what I was or how I was going to make it through another trial.

The closing arguments were to start in a couple of days. The closing argument was as devastating as the trial. As I listened, I felt I was about to die, but I couldn't, not just yet. The closing arguments lasted two days. That was two days of hell, two days I would never forget in my life.

The district attorney had complied all of his evidence together to convince the jurors that the defendant indeed murdered Kenny. We had to rehear a part of the doctor's, two witnesses, and the coroner's testimony. It was just too much. It ended and we had to wait two more weeks for the second trial to start. I left the courtroom feeling as though I had not accomplished anything. Kenny was dead.

The two weeks between the trials left me with very little to do. It left me crying and wanting to die. I felt I had done what I promised Kenny. I had at least seen the person who killed him. From what I had heard he would be punished, whether I lived or died. I was ready. I couldn't take it any longer. My heart was feeling heavy. The tears wouldn't stop, and I couldn't stay out of the cemetery long enough to make it through the next trial. Ending the trial and the closing arguments were enough to have killed me, yet I was still here.

Chapter 15
The Second Trial

Trial number two began exactly two weeks after the first trial ended. This one only lasted a week. Yet I had to see the same people over again. The doctors, the paramedics, the police officers, two of Kenny's friends and finally I got to see the co-defendant. I prayed to God that this one would end faster than the first trial. I knew if it would be longer I wasn't going to make it. I had already given up.

The trial started on Monday, and by Friday it was over. It was quicker and simpler, because he was just an accessory to the murder. I thanked God I never had to see the defendant again. He was the most arrogant, uncaring person I've ever seen. I was anxious to see the co-defendant as well.

I learned the gun used in the murder belonged to the co-defendant. He was no better than the defendant. I at least thought that. Entering the courtroom through the metal detectors, walking down the long hallway, gave me the same feeling I had two weeks ago.

We walked over to the court docket, looked for the co-defendant's name. I first spotted State/Kenny Smith vs. John Smith. I cried at the thought of his name appearing on the docket. We found the courtroom. We walked slowly; I wasn't ready and neither was my heart. I cried silently. I didn't want to go back into the courtroom again. I was tired now of the cold environment. Looking at the attorneys was aggravating. How can you represent someone you know killed someone? How? I guess everyone is innocent until proven guilty. I guess this person had a right. Even though Kenny had no rights. What right did I have? The anger began.

We entered the courtroom. It was a smaller one, which helped a lot. My understanding was this trial would be faster. I prayed it would be and it was. The co-defendant wasn't as arrogant as the defendant. He seemed to have a heart. He had no family members there to support him but a young girl around the age of seventeen. Who was at least eight months pregnant? It seemed no one cared, about the co-defendant or they were tired of being there for him. Whatever the case was I was tired too.

The judge came in and the same sound was heard, "All rise." I did as quickly as possible and sat down.

The first witness to the stand was the detective who secured the area where Kenny lay dying. He testified the exact same thing as in the first trial. Of course I expected him to but not the exact wording. You would have thought he had a tape recorder of his last testimony. Somehow his testimony ended rather quickly. I was glad.

He stepped down and the next witness to take the stand was the paramedic. My heart began to palpitate. I knew what she was about to say and didn't want to hear it, especially the part about Kenny being grave dead. How dare she. She did and there was nothing I could have done, she was doing her job. She did mention the fact that when she found Kenny he was grave dead. I still cried to hear her say that again. Even though I heard it before it didn't take away the pain.

I couldn't believe how fast this trial was going. I was hoping for another witness but instead it was time for lunch. I hated lunch. I wanted to keep going so when I left I could go home. The all too familiar saying court is adjourned made me want to scream. Instead all I could do was walk away.

I thanked God for my family. Many of them stood by me throughout the entire trial. We walked the halls together and we cried together. My mom was in the court with me every day. She was tired but she never left me. We walked over to the cafeteria and they ate. I was tired and wanted this to end.

I knew we had at least five more witness, plus the rebuttal. I prayed this would not take as long.

It was time to return to the courtroom. I was nervous. I walked in and took in a deep breath knowing we would get through at least two more witnesses, today. The judge returned late which didn't make it any better. It only gave me more time to sit and think. Think about who was going to be next. What he was going to say. Was it going to be exactly as before? I hoped not. The first testimony of some of the witnesses was long and drawn out and had a lot of detail.

The next person to testify was the doctor. I took in a deep breath. I knew what to expect. He still had a drawing board and pointer in his hand. He had a draft of injuries sustained in the shooting. He pointed out each wound and what effect it had. He was as detailed as he was during the first trial. He ended his testimony. I sighed with relief to know I never ever had to hear this testimony and never had to see the doctor again. Every time a witness stepped down I was relieved to know I never had to hear or see him again either. The doctor testified so long he was the last witness for the day. I prayed for at least one more but that was wishful thinking. The judge ended this until 9:00 a.m. I left the court praying that Friday would be over.

I went home and sat down and cried. I was tired of the testimony about Kenny. Kenny's death was too new in my heart for the on going testimony. I couldn't take it much longer, I didn't know if I was going to make it. I knew I had too; whether I was going to was another story. If it was left up to me I would die right now. It wasn't up to me, it was up to God. I knew he didn't bring me this far to leave me. I had to believe that. I tried all day to look up but it was hard. I knew it was almost over. I had to hold on.

The next morning came sooner than I wanted it to. It seemed as though the nights were getting shorter. I didn't sleep well last night. I tossed and turned half the night. I knew my husband was aggravated by me tossing and turning, but he never said anything. As soon as I seemed to have closed my eyes, the sun was coming up. Night seemed hard for me. I was afraid of the dark now. Darkness made me sad. It was dark when Kenny was shot and it was dark when he died. I wanted no part of the darkness for months.

I got up took a shower. I cried and cried as the water ran, asking God to please take me. I was tired. I stayed in the shower allowing it to beat down on me. I needed it. My body was tired. I reached over to shut off the water, yet the tears were flowing down to my chest. As soon as I dried off, I looked in the mirror. I didn't like what I saw. I saw a woman who wanted to die. A woman who was hurting, a woman who was sad, lost, and deep in pain. I looked up at the ceiling and asked God again as I have done so many times before, "Why?" No answer. I opened the bathroom door and went into the bedroom, and got dressed to go where I dreaded the most, the court.

To walk out the door was a struggle. It was getting colder which caused me even more stress. I knew we were at the end. It wasn't coming fast enough. My husband, my mom, my sister, my son and daughters, and a few of their friends headed to the court. Everyone seemed to be okay this morning not as tense as they have been. The co-defendant made our trip a little easier. I had begun to think okay.

The detective had been on, the paramedic had been on, the doctor had been on, so who was left? The two witnesses who were with Kenny. I prayed as I did before that they would do well, so we could end this trial. They did just that. They were able to have them both testify the same day. The young man who testified that Kenny dived through his car window was not in court; I was glad and sad at the same time.

The rebuttal was to begin on Friday. According to the prosecutor it should last no more than two days. I figured I had made it this far in more than two days, I would be okay. Thank God there was no court tomorrow. I didn't have to see this place again until Friday. I went home and took a deep breath.

I eased out of the house and headed to the cemetery to be with Kenny. I felt the need was there. I got in the car and hurriedly backed out before anyone missed me.

I got two blocks down the road and broke into tears. I cried and cried barely able to see the road. I knew where I was heading, whether I was going to make it was another story. The more I wiped my eyes the more tears poured down my face. My eyes felt so heavy, as though they were going to pop out of my head. I looked in the mirror and they were red and swollen. You couldn't see any of the white part of my eyes.

I continued to the cemetery. I could barely see the entrance but I made it. I drove up the hill. Pulled up next to Kenny's gravesite, turned off the car and cried my life away. I knew there were no sad faces, looking at me, no one to hide my screams from. I was in the middle of a cold cemetery. I laid my seat back and cried until I couldn't cry no more.

After I cried my heart out, I tried to open the car door. I was too weak. Before getting out I looked in the mirror. I looked a mess, I felt a mess. I didn't care anymore. I wanted to talk to Kenny. I wanted to let him know it was almost over.

I opened the door and got out. I could barely see for my eyes being so swollen. I walked over to his gravesite and kneeled down and begin crying again. I said, "I miss you so much." I told him, "We're almost at the end. I'm keeping my promise as I told you. We have one more day."

I tried to get up, but my I couldn't. My body was too weak. I had to lean against the tombstone next to Kenny to get up. What I really wanted to do was lay my body next to Kenny. All kind of things were going through my mind. I wanted to dig up his grave and bury myself in their with him. I was losing it.

I walked over to my car open the door and grabbed on to the steering wheel and pulled myself in the car. I shut the door and lay back in the seat and continued to cry. I knew it was getting dark and I needed to leave the cemetery. I turned on the ignition and proceeded to drive only to realize I was looking back at Kenny's gravesite and almost drove off the sidewalk. I exited the entrance side of the cemetery. I looked both ways and saw no others cars, yet when I pulled out I heard a loud screeching sound. I was almost hit by another car. It was God who saved me. I had no care in the world. I hunched my shoulders and continued to drive, not even paying attention. If only the driver of the other car knew what was on my mind.

I knew my family was looking for me. I was going to be asked where I was. I stopped by the grocery store. I picked up a few items. This was going to be my alibi. I hurried into the store and out as quickly as possible. I knew I had been gone for three hours. What I brought didn't take three hours. I didn't care anymore. On the drive home all I could think about was Kenny was dead and I couldn't believe it.

I pulled into the driveway. As soon as I turned off the engine I saw a body move the curtain. It was my youngest, Starla. She opened the door and asked me where I had been. I said to the store and my other daughter Julia said that long. I never looked up. If I had looked up they would have surely seen I had been crying. My eyes were swollen. I made it past the children, but my husband noticed my eyes. He asked where I had been and I told him to the store. I let him think what he wanted to.

I went into the bathroom and put a cold towel on my face. Hoping to take down some of the puffiness in my eyes. I stayed in the bathroom for about ten minutes before someone knocked on the door.

The trial was winding down. It was the end of what had been a long and drawn out ordeal. My inner body was happy. Happy there were no more courtrooms, no more doctors, no more paramedics. It was a relief, finally, after a total of six months of pure hell. My body cried because it couldn't take any more.

Just to walk out of the courtroom and not to look back was a blessing. I knew I only had one more trip back to the court. I dreaded it. I cried. I said, "No God I can't take any longer." I made it.

The last of the two trials ended on Wednesday. Not like the first one which ended on a Friday. Friday is a very sad day for me. Friday was the day Kenny was shot and was the day Kenny died.

The attorney told me I would be notified of the sentencing date.

The wait was over sooner than I expected. It was worth it, even though no one won. One parent's child was murdered and the other parent lost a child to prison.

I had two weeks to wait for the sentencing. Still my life couldn't go on. I had to face the murderer and co-murderer. What other way could I possibly say it. I didn't return to work yet. I was not yet ready to face the world. I felt I had already shut myself off and I was not ready to turn it back on. I knew there were a lot of people who cared about me. There were a lot of people who had children that could not feel my pain. I felt I had to be strong for them. I knew if I cried they would have too. I couldn't cry anymore. I was tired of crying.

Two weeks came fast. Before I realized it I was back at the place I hated the most, the courtroom. It was filled with family and friends on both sides. All of us seemed to be afraid. I was afraid he might get off. It can happen, if you look at enough television. The defendant's mother was afraid her son would spend his life in jail. Either way we both were going to hurt. I sighed for a moment. Thought about my promise to Kenny and held my mom's hand tight. I knew she understood my fear. I was like a child afraid. I wanted this day to end, but not before the sentencing.

The door to the left came opened and the face I dreaded the most entered the courtroom. The defendant, the murderer, the person who destroyed my life stood before the judge and jurors, still showing no signs of emotion. The foreman was taking forever to read the verdict. Before reading it he handed it to the judge. The judge motioned the defendant to stand. He asked him did he have anything he wanted to say to the family. He said, "No." How could he show no emotions?

I looked into the eyes of a monster child, able to kill with no remorse and I wondered if he had a heart. No reaction did he show as the verdict was read. I even thought this would one day be a decision he would come to dread. He took a part of my life and I was no longer whole. He took a part of my very soul. My child, no longer able to run, live, or even see, and this monster acted like this was the way it was supposed to be. A mother, just like me, what could his mother be feeling to know that a part of her was now a killer? A taker of God's most precious gift, life. He had no care for me and mine but what about those who are a part of him? Inside did he ever ask how or why could he be responsible for taking a life?

In the still of the night when quiet is all around, did he regret the decision that put my son into the ground? Surely he thought about how much my heart must ache, the sound it makes as it slowly breaks into a thousand pieces. Yes I looked into the eyes of a monster child and for a moment in time I truly despised this person. I know that it was not God's will for me to feel this bitterness, but I could not help what my heart felt at that moment.

I knew in time I would be able to truly find peace, but even today, I have to say, I am still searching for that moment. I miss my child and the things we could have done. I miss the opportunity to see what he could have become. I think back to yesterday and I feel afraid of the feelings that claimed me. I know now I am only human. No one but God has the right to take a life. A life for a life, but is it really fair when his parents and family can see him still living even though he's in jail? If I could see my son and touch him even if it was from heart to heart, what a difference that would make to me. I will never be able to see the expression on his face as I tell him about his children growing up and all that they are and all that they may become. It hurts because he was more than my son, he was my best friend. I lost my best friend on January 5, 1990, someone I watched grow up into a handsome young man. I had so many hopes for him that will never be able to come true and I ask you; is any of this fair?

He stood with no care in the world. For once I stared him right in his eyes. He showed no emotion. Couldn't he hear my heart breaking? The sound was so loud that I could hear. I thought angrily how could he show no feeling, and then I remembered here was a child who had no value to life. He took a part of my life and I knew even then that one day, whether it be today or tomorrow, he would cry for his life.

The courtroom was quiet as sentencing was read. The judge sentenced him to life plus forty years. How could he not show any emotions?

There is no way you could convince me some part of him, was not affected by the sentencing. It affected me, not because I was Kenny' mother, but because I am a human being. I cared about his family. If he didn't move a muscle for Kenny, what about his mother. She too had lost a son. The verdict ended and two sets of parents walked away empty handed. No one won. We both lost something. But she had a little more than I did. She could go to the jail and visit her son; I had to go the cemetery.

My family and I walked out of the courtroom, hoping never to return. Yet we had one more trip to make. The co-defendant had to be sentenced. My life still couldn't move forward yet. We left the courtroom, but not with a victory.

The first day after the sentencing, I cried all day. I cried for many reasons. I cried because I was glad it was over, I cried because I had to now live my life without my child, I cried because I didn't know what to do, I cried because I felt I was alone, I cried because I was afraid, I cried because I didn't understand why Kenny had to die. I cried because God let Kenny die, I cried because I no longer had to see the faces of the murderer, and I cried because I had cried silently for days, weeks and months.

I cried for days, week's months and years; that's why God chose me to share this with you. I wondered how I survived. How was I going to be a mother, a wife, a sister, a daughter, an aunt, and a grandmother? I survived and I thanked God every day. I thank God for all he has done for me. I said all and I mean all. I owe it all to him. I struggled not because I wanted to but because of the pain. It was devastating, the fear was devastating, and the surrounding was devastating. And life itself was devastating.

The ride home was a relief for the family, but just the beginning for me. I had to learn how to survive after the death of my child. I felt I had a hard road ahead of me. I was not looking forward to it. I had another trip to the cemetery. I had to let Kenny know it was almost over. I didn't care any more who knew where I was going or where I'd been.

I drove to the cemetery. I got out of my car and went over to Kenny' gravesite. I kneeled down to tell him, "Baby, it's almost over." I was choking in tears and pain. I didn't stay long this time.

After the trial was another new beginning, a new life, a new everything. I had to adjust again. A life without my son. I couldn't begin to imagine, I didn't want to either. Yet I had very little choice. Life with my children, life with my husband, a life I had known so well, yet I felt so lost. Lost in shame, pity, confusion, anger, and pain so deep. I wondered if I would survive. I didn't think I would even though I had a loving family. That didn't take away the pain I endured after Kenny's death.

I didn't know where to begin. All I knew was the life I had in front of me was not the life I wanted to live. I know if I had a choice death would be one. I sat on the side of the bed contemplating suicide. I felt I had no reason to go on. No reason to get up, no reason to wake up, no reason to eat, no reason to sleep.

There's no reason for anything after the death of a child. My body felt heavy; heavy from the burden we call grief. My body hurt so bad the most I could do the day after the trial was lay my tired, aching body across the bed, hoping and praying not to wake up. It wasn't my choice so I had to remember God was in control. Even though a part of me was still angry with God. A part of me was still trying to believe. Believe that God made no mistakes. That was the hardest thing in my life, trying to believe again.

I begin trying to live again. It was yes one day, no the next day, the day after why, what was there to live for? There was no answer, only one question I asked myself. What had I done in my life to go through such a tragedy? I realized later that's why I went through what I did, because God chose me to. And when God calls, you have no choice.

Chapter 16
Marriage After the Death of a Child

My marriage was deteriorating day by day. I became so distant with my husband. I couldn't stand for him to hold me. It hurt too bad. My body was in pain too deep for a hug. He never understood the loneliness I was going through. Yes we lived in the same house, slept in the same bed. But yet he never understood. He felt after a couple of months had gone, by my life was supposed to return to normal. That can't happen and didn't happen. I needed time to grieve. I never took time in the beginning. I was too busy denying Kenny's death. I couldn't believe. I went to sleep, just hoping to wake up to a bad dream. I woke up many a night believing it was a dream, only to realize it was not a dream. Kenny was gone and gone forever. It hurt so bad. There were times all I could do was kneel on the floor and cry and ask God Why? I knew Kenny didn't deserve to die; I didn't deserve to be grieving like this. God knew through it all there would be peace in the midst of the storm. A storm was what I was in.

A marriage takes a beating, no one wins and no one loses. You become very distant with each other. You tend to lay blame on each other. My marriage became unbearable.

My husband wanted life to return to normal, not realizing your life can never be the same. I hid the pain, because I didn't think he understood. Instead of turning to him, I turned away. We became strangers in our home.

I looked back over the years and I truly see why a marriage of ten years disappeared. I loved my husband and we shared many beautiful moments together before Kenny's death. At one point we were inseparable. Now all I want to do is to be alone. I felt we couldn't go on like this.

At night he would turn over wanting to have sex, but I couldn't, I needed to just be held. I cried and felt it was wrong for me to smile, to be happy, to eat to sleep. Kenny was dead and so was a part of me. How was I going to hold on to my marriage?

My husband said he couldn't understand my grieving so long, everybody has to die. I understood that but that was no consolation. It was only about his sexual needs. His needs were not a concern to me. I had a dead child and I was dying. He didn't want to hear that.

For six months after Kenny's death, I spent every evening in the cemetery crying. I don't think my husband would have understood or even tried to understand. I was no longer a wife. I couldn't perform my duties as his wife. That was when our marriage began going down hill. I needed more than sex. I needed to be held, to be understood, to fall asleep in each other's arm without the intimacy of sex. He seemed not to be able to separate the two. He felt his way of consoling me was through sex. No sex led to arguments, harsh words which can never be forgotten.

He told me I never cared about him. I only cared about Kenny. I screamed silently. He would often come in from work. I would be crying, he would look at me and walk into the kitchen and get a beer and go upstairs and watch television. I needed him so bad. All I needed was a hug. He couldn't give me that without wanting sex. I told him I wanted nothing more than to be held, and he said that was impossible. I felt if he had tried to love me in a different way, we could have gotten through this. Before Kenny's death I was a good wife, provider in all ways. I just didn't have it anymore.

Each time with his harsh words, we became more distant day by day. He turned the kids to believe I didn't love them, that all I loved was Kenny. That wasn't true. I love my children. I would have done anything and I did everything to be there for them. I may not have been the cheerful mother they had always known but I was the best mother I could have been under the circumstances. I didn't drink, I didn't do drugs. I did grieve, but not by choice. He wasn't the nicest person to me anymore, since I could no longer do my wifely duties. Through my silent tears I said, "I love you and the children."

His response was, "Well you don't show it."

"Why, because I cannot have sex with you?" I needed more than sex at this point of my life and he couldn't provide me with that. He felt the only way to show love is through sex. He knew before Kenny's death, I never refused him. I was hurting deeper than he would ever know. He felt I had grieved enough. Kenny was my child. Who has the right to tell me when grieving is enough.

I thought my husband was my best friend. I later found out through the death of my child he was a typical asshole and cared about nothing about me other than when I could provide his sexual needs. He told me many times I don't know how to deal with death. Again that was my child. I asked him "How do you deal with death?

He said, "You let go and move on." This is why I let go and I moved on. We divorced. I couldn't believe it at that moment all I knew was Kenny was dead and I was dying. My youngest daughter Starla asked her daddy why he was so mean. He told her, "If I hadn't been mean she would have been worse off than she was."

She asked him, "Why would you throw fuel in the fire? You only made her hate you more."

He said, "Our marriage is the way it is because of Kenny dying." That was a blow in the chest. I cried.

I prayed that God would give my husband the strength and the knowledge to be able to understand that when a child dies, it takes a part of you. A part of you is ripped away.

Many years passed by and I was not getting any better. He got angrier and more impatient. We became distant to each other. I would sit up in the living room half the night before going to bed. He wanted sex; I couldn't and he began refusing to pay the bills in the house. He said to me, "You can't do anything for me, why should I give you anything?" I cried silently and walked away.

This was where I became mentally closed in and independent. I knew now it was about me surviving an abusive husband and the death of a child. I hid this from the children. Now I had two burdens on me; trying to survive this grief that was killing me and a husband who didn't give a damn.

It became harder day after day for me to live. For one, without the financial support from him there was a crisis in the home, since there were four other children to take care of. That was when I gained my strength. My children needed me and I couldn't let them down. He paid the rent and, as far as he was concerned, that was the end of his responsibility. I put my grief on the back burner and gave him what he wanted everything got paid. Afterwards I would turn over and cry. I wasn't ready. I have four children that needed to be taken care of.

I felt as though I had to become a prostitute for my own husband. I cried many a night afterwards because I was hurting for affection, not sex. His drinking increased so he became more forceful. I accepted his sexual abuse for as long as I could. Forget the affection, forget the communication, forget anything about me. I know he missed the relationship we had and so did I.

I just wanted to get better. He gave me no reason to hold on. He wanted life to be as it was before Kenny died and so did I. But only time would allow that to happen. He didn't have time.

He began working late hours. I guess he felt, What was at home but a grieving wife? He said to me one day, "You are always so uptight all the time. Why don't you take a drink?"

I said, "Why would I want to do that?"

He said, "You would feel better." Looking at him, I knew that wasn't true.

I said, "If I start drinking and you're already drinking, who is going to take care of the children?" I refused to drink and he got upset.

Our marriage never returned to normal. I began to get stronger and I didn't forget the things he said to me. I tried to begin to perform my duties as wife. But this time when I did it was cold. I felt it was now a chore. A chore I didn't want to do. He became a stranger in my bedroom.

I hope you never have to experience the death of a child, but if you do don't let no one tell you how long you should grieve. Take the time you need because if you don't do it now you will have to one day.

May God bless all of the husbands and wives who remember, death is very painful and everyone grieves differently. Be patient with your spouse.

Days and nights I spent alone in my bedroom, hiding from the world. I couldn't let anyone know how bad I was hurting. I was too embarrassed, why I don't know. I thought I was supposed to be strong for everyone. I had every reason to scream, lie on the ground and cry forever. It was my child who was murdered.

It took me nine years and three months, and I truly thank God. I didn't think I was going to live through the first year. So many angels God had planted around me to take care of me. I know it had to be God's work. The devil was trying to kill me. He wanted me dead. He didn't want me to help you, to know that you too can survive after the death of a child, a mother, father, sister, brother, husband, and wife. He wanted to kill, steal and destroy. The devil wanted to kill me. For a year he was killing me slowly. I was allowing him to, not by choice but because I knew no other way to live. How was I supposed to have live after the death of my child?

I was grieving myself to death. Grief is like the devil it comes to kill, steal and destroy. Grief will kill you. So many people die every day from grief. Grief is like a silencer on a gun, it will kill you without leaving a trace. Grief will have you crying and not even knowing why. Grief is a dangerous, addictive substance. Once in your body, you have to ask God to remove and mean it.

My body was grief stricken. It had a hold of me so bad until I knew nothing but to keep my head down, crying feeling sorry for myself, contemplating suicide, angry with God, angry with the world and angry with myself.

Grief is an addiction. It's like drugs. You feel almost a need to be down, feeling sorry for yourself. My husband never understood that grief had control of me. I was grieving day in and day out. I sometimes didn't understand myself. He would get angry with me. He didn't understand grief either.

Chapter 17
Ten Years Later

I thought this was the end. There is never an end to surviving after the death of a child. You learn to live with it. I would have given my life to think that after ten years the wound would be closed a little. My heart is tired. I had no choice but to go on. At times it hurt as though it was yesterday. I cry sometimes as though it was yesterday. This year I spent the anniversary of Kenny's death in hiding. I still feel after ten years I can't let anyone know I still hurt. I've learned over the years there's nothing wrong with that.

Chapter 18
Spiritual Relapse

My faith was gone. I fought for days, weeks, months and years to understand why God let Kenny die. I felt if there was truly a loving God and understanding God where was he when Kenny died? Especially when I was told all you had to do was pray. I prayed harder than I ever had for Kenny, but God let me down. I couldn't understand.

I lost my faith on January 5, 1990. That was the day Kenny died. A part of me went with him. A part that stayed buried with him for eight years. I buried a part of me into him. I couldn't pray anymore. I lost the will to live. I felt I was slipping, I was dying and I no longer cared. I was angry with God for not allowing me to die. I felt staying here was punishing me. How was I going to live? I felt if I couldn't trust God who could I trust? I had buried my child and gone through two trials and yet I couldn't understand there had to be a God. If there wasn't how was I still living through this? I should have been dead after Kenny died. I had no desire to live. I wanted more than anything to die. I couldn't.

I guess a part of me believed there was a God and a part of me believed there wasn't. I lay in bed many a night crying and asking God why? I lost valuable time, time I can never get back. I was a believer, I know God, I knew how powerful God is. I knew if I was going to make it, it would be through the grace of god. Yet I would not pray. I couldn't call his name. I was too angry. I stopped going to church. I felt there was no reason to go to church.

On March 21, 1991, I went to church. I was tired of crying, tired of hurting, and tired of the sleepless nights, tired of running no where. My body couldn't take it anymore. I don't recall planning to go to church. I was going to church alone. I was crying, still hurting. I felt everyone was looking at me. I didn't care. I walked in the church the usher handed me a program. I walked slowly down the isle and found a seat close to the end of the aisle in the event I had to leave. I felt like a stranger in the house of the Lord. I knew that was what the devil wanted me to believe. He put me on the end of the seat because he wanted me to leave.

In spite of all the reasons the whys, the yeses, and the no's I stayed there. I knew I had been down long enough. I wanted help. I knew I had to want it. The choir began singing and I begin crying silently, then openly. I remember the usher came over and a gave me a tissue. I figured the tears I was sharing were tears of joy. I felt so at peace.

I continued listening to the choir sing. They began to pray. God knew my pain, the loneliness in my body. That was all that mattered. While people were around me praising him I remain quiet, but observant. I felt maybe they had something to praise God for. I still felt angry, unsure as to the belief of praying. People were shouting and saying over and over thank you Jesus. I couldn't understand why. I felt sad. I do remember the pastor coming in. He was shouting and had the entire congregation on their feet, including me.

He said, "If you have anything to thank God for stand up." I don't know why I was standing. A part of me asked why I was standing. That was Satan. I stood anyway. I felt at one point the devil was sitting right next to me. I had a little faith. I guess that was all I needed. He wasn't going to steal my faith today. He had me long enough. I was tired. I continued to stand as long as I could.

The pastor said, "Sit down if you can." I didn't want to. I wanted to run to the front of the church and stretch my body across the altar. I wanted to scream openly for the first time.

I wanted to live again. I wanted not to cry every day. I needed peace. I had been in the storm for to long. The same pastor who married me was about to bury me and didn't even know it. Then again maybe he did know it.

After preaching he came down the aisle as usual for the benediction, opening his arms to who ever needed or wanted to turn their life around? He walked the floor back and forth. Repeating God cares, and he knows what you're going through. I sat even tighter in my seat. I knew I wasn't ready. Nothing was going to change my mind. He continued walking, opening his hands for anyone. The choir was singing very low. He said, "Shh!" The choir stopped singing, the church got quiet. He said, "There's someone in here who's been battling with something for a while now. You've tried your way. God told me to tell you to give it up; it's time to let go and let God. I don't know who you are, but God told me to tell you this." I stood up in tears and walked down the aisle crying. I knew how bad I had been hurting. I knew this was my call. He ended his benediction and I began my life with God. I knew I had made the right choice. I just know I did.

I left church, went home and called my mother. I knew if anyone cared she did. She prayed for me more than I prayed for myself. My mom was tired, tired of seeing her daughter dying slowly, tired of not being able to help me. She tried everything in her power to save me. I knew she would be happy. She knew she had a chance, to help me because I helped myself. I remember when I told her she said over and over again, "Thank you, Jesus." She knew I would be saved from the devil. She knew God would watch over me and he did.

The change didn't happen overnight. I still endured some hard times, sad times, crying times. The good part about it is I knew that as long as I knew God everything was going to be alright. I trusted him again. I knew I had to believe in order to receive what God had for me. My nights were still lonely, but in the midnight hour instead of crying I prayed. A part of me was still hurting, a part of me would never understand why Kenny had to die.

I started going to church on a regular basis. I buried myself in church. I felt if I was going to hide behind anybody it was going to be God. I had already tried to do it myself and I made a mess out of it.

What I would like to share with each of you who has taken the time to read this book, is that God is the only one. You hear me? I mean the only one. Who is going to be able to give you peace in the midst of this storm? After the death of a child some of us try running away from the problems. The problems will not go away until you come to Jesus. It's going to be hard to trust in him and he knows how you feel. Alcohol isn't going to help you, drugs can't help you, man can't help you, and momma can't help. Come to Jesus.

He healed my body. Not overnight but in time, when I most needed it. I had already gone through two trials. Though I went in with no faith and no trust and you know what, I almost died. At least I thought I did. I sat in the courtroom angry with the person who killed Kenny, and a God who I felt let Kenny die. I had a double dose of anger. I knew God understood. I knew in the end God would get the glory; the glory was me giving my life back to him.

Chapter 19
Siblings

I never knew the pain a child suffers after the death of a sibling. I felt the children were too young to understand. I later found out they hurt just as bad as the parents. They feel the loss, pain, sadness and sorrow and lost of hope. My children never expressed their sorrow because they were to busy protecting me, as I had been them. They wanted to be strong for me. Many a night they sat on the side of the bed and watched me cry helplessly. That was a side of me they saw. A side of me I never let them see again. I've always been a shoulder for them to lean on and to dry their tears. I needed them and they were there. I felt so helpless. We all shared a loss. I lost a son, they lost a brother.

My children were always and have been my best friends. And we all lost a best friend when Kenny died. I knew they were going through something. I had nothing to offer. I could barely help myself. I took them to get professional help. My children were hurting. I just figured children didn't understand. Children are people, they hurt too. I wish a many days I could have done more. I couldn't.

I called their doctor. I needed to get them into counseling. They needed help. Help I couldn't give them. I didn't know what to do. I got the nurse on the telephone. I explained to her I needed to make an appointment for my children. She asked what seemed to be the problem. I told her my son had been murdered and my children were grieving silently. They wouldn't open up to me. I was hoping someone could reach them. She gave me an appointment the next day. I was afraid, I didn't know what to expect, how were they going to talk to a stranger?

I told them I had made an appointment for them to talk to someone about how they were feeling since Kenny's death. They said they didn't want to talk to anyone. This time I understood, yet I knew I had to do something. I told them, "Let's try anyway." My son was very reluctant to go to counseling.

He said, "Why talk to her? Did her son die?" I told him I didn't know. He wasn't ready to talk; he was angry.

We went to the doctor's office. I had to fill out four sets of forms. I tried to hear what they were talking about. I finished the paper work and handed it to the receptionist. She looked up after reading the paper, and then walked to the back, and within minutes she was coming back. She called each of them by their name. They laughed and I was glad to see them smile for a change.

While in the back I told them not to be afraid to tell the doctor how they felt. My daughter Julia said, "I don't want to talk to her." I tried to her it was for the best that they talk to someone. She got angry and wanted to know why they had to. I begged her to tell the doctor what she was feeling. The door came opened and they all looked up, then at each other sadly, as though what am I going to say. The doctor introduced herself. She started by saying, "Who's the oldest?" Of course Shundra raised her hand. "Who's next to the oldest?" Julius and Julia raised their hands. She asked, "Now how can both of you be the next to the oldest?"

They said, "We're twins."

"Who's the oldest twin?"

Julius said, "I'm the oldest by ten minutes."

She looked at Starla, "And I guess you must be the youngest." Starla nodded her head yes. I thanked God at least they were talking.

She asked who wanted to be the first one to tell why they were here. The room got so quiet; you would have thought it was empty. I looked at them picking at their hands, they began to cry. Shundra spoke up, choking out the words she missed her big brother, and she couldn't understand why someone would kill him and she cried harder. The doctor handed her a tissue. She told Shundra it was okay to miss Kenny, he could still be close to her in spirit, she didn't quite understand that and really I don't think she was trying to hear that, at least not right then.

When she finished, Shawn said, "But Kenny was the best brother in the world." I went over to her and hugged her, crying silently myself I tried to hold back the tears.

Julius spoke, saying he couldn't understand either why they killed his brother. He was a little stronger. He fought back the tears. He said over and over, "Kenny should not have died." He said, "I even miss him more because we shared the same bedroom and sometimes the same bed if it was cold." I thought that was really a bond. He played with his hands and said, "I miss him so much." I had already moved closer to all of them. I grabbed his hand and held it tightly. Within minutes they were all crying including me.

It was now Julia's turned to speak, which I already knew was not going to happen. She said nothing she cried the entire time. The doctor asked if she had anything to say and she said, "No" and continued to cry. I opened my hands and held hers. All that could come out of her mouth is, "I miss him." She began to cry openly.

The last was Starla, my six year old daughter. She didn't quite understand what was going on, when asked how she was dealing with all of this she hunched her shoulders and played with her hand. She had nothing to say.

The session ended for the day. I felt there was some accomplishment because on the way home they were talking and laughing. I looked up and whispered to God, "Thank you." Remember, children hurt just as bad as we do.

Time went by and we continued to struggle everyday to make it. We all learned to take one minute at a time. One day seemed too hard. It became harder for me every second. They pretended to return to a somewhat normal life while I continued to struggle to find mine. As time went by they began to open up by telling me I made them feel like Kenny was the only child. Never did I intend to make any of them feel that way. When death comes sudden it's harder. I loved each one of them in a special way. I wanted them to be a little more understanding. They couldn't and I understood. I had to find myself again. I had to learn how to be a mother again.

I say to every parent who has experienced the death of a child don't shut out the other children. Pray and ask God to cover them with his blood.

They said they couldn't go back to the doctor's office again. I understood why they couldn't and wouldn't come back. It was hard to talk about such a loving brother and son who had died so violently.

I stopped by McDonalds to feed them. We sat and talked, not about Kenny. I was sitting physically, but mentally I was somewhere else.

They finished eating and we left. I got home and went upstairs and sat on the bed. I tried to tell my husband he should have gone with us. He wouldn't talk about him either. If and whenever he did he was under the influence of alcohol. That was when I found it the hardest time to talk to him.

Closure for me has been very hard. A many days and nights I lay across my bed wondering God could there be a closure to such pain. I thought I had to at some point close this book. As much as and as many times as I've tried and I cried. I thought for a second closure meant letting go of Kenny. Even though it has been over 10 years. At some point I still feel I'm holding on. That's okay. I have every right to hold on to the memories. That's all I had left. There is no more feeling, touching, seeing Kenny. It's hard to close this chapter of my life but I must. I close this book giving God all the glory. I know if it wasn't for God I wouldn't be here today. As I said so many times before I wanted to give up, but God said, "No." He comforted my broken heart in the midnight hour. The nights I lay crying, wanting every second to let go. I thank God for healing me. After the death of a child you will have to go through something.

The years I lost, I can't get back. I missed being the mom, the wife, the sister the aunt I used to be ten years ago. I can't do anything about that but ask God to continue healing me, so that I can be me.

Being me is hard enough. Being anything else other than me requires the help of God.

Closing this chapter of my life has been an experience that I never want to do again. I still have for four children, and two step children. I pray that at no point in the rest of my life will I have to walk this road again. I pray that before I have to bury any more of my children, I have gone home to be with the lord. I can't do it again.

Anything you do without God in your life will be a challenge. You can't survive without the Grace if God. I cried today, I felt lonely I needed somebody to just give me a hug. The pain is deep in my body. I still scream silently.

To all of you that have felt my pain, I want you to know there is light at the end of the tunnel. It's a long road but believe me God will see you through.

To all the parents of a murdered child, I extend my condolence to you. May God be with you and protect you as he did me. There are going to be days you're going to feel no one understands how bad you feel, always remember God does and so do I.

God has blessed me. My children are all grown now. My oldest daughter Shundra, who always have been the strongest of the girls, is now thirty-four, Julia and Julius are now thirty-one and my baby Starla is now twenty-four. I have eight grandchildren whom I love dearly. Lil Kenny seventeen, Shanae sixteen, Shakia fifteen, Ashleigh fifteen, Branden fifteen, Brittany twelve, Quesean ten and my dear baby Heavyn two. I have two sons-in-law, Tony and Barry, and one daughter-in-law, Angie. I know I sound like an obituary.

I thank God for my children. They are my reasons for living.

Chapter 20
Thirteen Years Later

It has been thirteen years today that I have to again remember the saddest day of my life. December 29. I prayed the night before to God to watch over me. I tried, I cried silently throughout my workday. Even though I smiled with my co-workers, I cried silently. The thought that one of the boys who shot Kenny was celebrating a birthday. I was crying just for a day to see Kenny. The thought of his family able to send him a card, hear his voice or even visit him. What did I have? Nothing but sad memories of Kenny.

I wanted more than anything just to hear him one more time. The thought that I couldn't made me cry silently. At one point I felt a tear in my eye, which let me know my cries were not as silent as I thought they were.

I spent the day alone. I wondered if anyone else remembered what day it was or did it really matter to anyone other than me? I felt alone, as I have been for years. I wanted to cry but what good would it do? Instead of crying I sat in front of my computer. I stared up at the wall where a large 11x23 picture hangs in my living room and smiled at the picture of Kenny. I looked into his eyes and all I saw was a handsome guy with light brown eyes, with a loving heart, who wouldn't hurt anyone. I rubbed the picture and began to cry to him. I really miss him so much. Tears continued to roll down my face. My eyes began to burn from the mascara I wore on my eyes today. The burn couldn't be as bad as how I was feeling.

The children are all grown up now. Everyone has his or her own family now. I have no one but God and me. I no longer have my mother, who I know today would understand my cry.

This is a trying time for me. I've learned to depend on the one and only God. My tears could only be dried through him. What I would like to have happen today is for my children to help me through the day by all of us going out to dinner, taking me away from the sadness that's enduring in my heart. Instead no one even called to say, "Hi, Mom, how are you doing?" It seems as though everyone now has their own family and they have moved on. Everyone seemed to but me. I don't know why I expected anything different. How many times have I asked myself, how many times have I been through this expecting someone to hear my cries. Thirteen years have gone, and I still feel sad. I never thought I would be able to move on. The pain, the sadness, the loneliness, the loss of hope, the suicidal thoughts.

My life has been stricken a little by an illness. I don't know for sure the reason, neither do the doctors. I read an article on it that states it may come from emotional stress. If that is the case I can very well understand why I have what I have. I know if I made it through the death of my child, God will surely pull me through this. I cried when I realized that I had not done what God had asked me to do, which is to help you through the death of your child. I never gave up but sometimes it just seemed no one cared. Yet children are dying through violence every day.

I knew it was time when the Million-Mom-March took place. It was a wake up call for me. I knew it was time for me to help God's people. I cried silently to know that all these people are hurting, going through the pain, suffering, the loneliness I know only God will see them through. I read an article where mothers were crying out, telling their stories for the first time. I cried with them. I understood their cry. I asked God for the strength to get over the writers block, which was the devil. I felt there were too many Kennys and does anyone care about Kenny? The answers is yes, someone cares about Kenny. There were many Kennys at the Million-Mom-March.

Looking at the faces of those crying moms made me realize again I miss Kenny so much. Never a day has gone by, that I didn't miss him.

This Million-Mom-March broke my heart all over again. It wasn't as broken as it was thirteen years ago. I gave it to God. I know he watched over me in the midst of the Million-Mom-March was on May 14. As much as I would have wanted to be there my health wouldn't allow me. My heart was there and my ear was there to hear all the cries of moms who lost their children to senseless murders. All I could say was, "Dear God."

Chapter 21
Look Back, Don't Fall Back

Many days, nights, months, and years I looked back and I fell back. It was harder each time to get up. I couldn't help but to look back. I couldn't see forward. The thought of Kenny dead caused me to fall back each time. Not that I wanted to, but because it hurt so badly, it knocked me back. Every time I fell it seemed as though I was becoming a part of whatever I fell on. Many days I felt like a chair, I sometimes felt like a doormat. Sometimes I felt like nothing. Yet I continued to fall into pity. It's okay you can do that. No one knows the pain I was going through but God. He's the only one who knows the pain associated with falling back after the death of a child. I tried for weeks to type, and each time it got harder and I cried silently. The thought of the times I spent falling back has helped me to appreciate looking forward. Sometimes I find my self reminiscing over what I should have, or could have had. I realize that whatever I didn't get while grieving was not meant for me. I look back sometimes and say to myself, "What if Kenny hadn't died?" Would I have the car I wanted? Would I have had a big house? I grieved so long that time passed me by. I feel so sad sometimes when I look back over my life, but its okay. I know whatever God has for me it will be mine forever. Sometimes I have to remember it wasn't my time for those things. Sometimes I often wondered, if Kenny hadn't died where, would I be. Sometimes there are no answers.

Deep within my heart I still ask myself what could I have done differently. I blamed myself for Kenny not being here, knowing all the time I had nothing to do with pulling the trigger that killed Kenny.

Revenge could never replace Kenny. I want more anything in this world to face the person who killed Kenny, one more time, even though I saw him for two weeks at the trial. My feeling was different then than now. I was numb, still in shock. I've had time to think now with a somewhat clear mind. Not a trial, in front of me.

In that time of my life I didn't know who I was, where I was going. All I knew was that I had a promise to fulfill, the promise I made to Kenny on his death bed, to make sure who ever did this to him would pay. I had to do it. I did. I thank God for the strength he gave me to hold on.

Even if you have not been to court because they have been unable to find the person who is responsible, don't give up; continue to pray; pray harder than you ever have. Ask God to watch over you, guide you, and protect you through it all. I know you want some kind of closure; there is no closure, but there is life after the death of a child.

May God Bless and protect you through your time of sorrow. I am a survivor after the death of my child, and I want you to be too.

Another Beginning

A special thanks to a special friend, Allaine. Thanks for re-typing and editing *A Silent Scream*. It was hard for me to relive those moments. Thanks for stepping in and doing what was impossible for me. I couldn't have done this without you.

Those long hours finally paid off. The trips to the library researching, and late nights on the internet were overwhelming. In spite of your loss of your daughter Nickii, you allowed it to be only about Kenny and my goals to get *A Silent Scream* published. I hope and pray *A Silent Scream* can bring you comfort in your loss and lets you know that you are not alone. May Kenny and Nickii rest in peace.

Your Friend
May God Bless
A special thanks to my mom.
I LOVE YOU

Printed in the United States
119492LV00001BA/186/A

9 781424 192519